THE CHURCH AND ENGLISH LIFE

THE CHURCH
AND ENGLISH LIFE

SERMONS

BY THE RIGHT REVEREND

BERTRAM POLLOCK, D.D., K.C.V.O.

LORD BISHOP OF NORWICH

LONGMANS, GREEN AND CO.

LONDON · NEW YORK · TORONTO

1932

LONGMANS, GREEN AND CO. LTD.

39 PATERNOSTER ROW, LONDON, E.C.4.
6 OLD COURT HOUSE STREET, CALCUTTA
53 NICOL ROAD, BOMBAY
36A MOUNT ROAD, MADRAS

LONGMANS, GREEN AND CO.

55 FIFTH AVENUE, NEW YORK
221 EAST 20TH STREET, CHICAGO
88 TREMONT STREET, BOSTON
128–132 UNIVERSITY AVENUE, TORONTO

MADE IN GREAT BRITAIN

DEDICATED

BY GRACIOUS PERMISSION

TO

H.R.H.
THE DUKE OF CONNAUGHT

CONTENTS

PART II. THE ENGLISH CHURCH : YOUTH AND EDUCATION

PART III. DOCTRINE IN THE ENGLISH CHURCH

PART IV. WORSHIP

PREFACE

I HAVE to express my respectful gratitude to H.R.H. the Duke of Connaught for graciously accepting the dedication of this volume. In the days when I was Master of Wellington College I had the honour of serving under him. Though he is in no way responsible for anything that I have written, I cannot but think that a book, which in parts deals with the rearing of the young, is fortunate to possess on its title-page the name of a Prince who, after his own long life of devotion to duty, has it in his heart to evoke a spirit of unselfish service from the rising generation.

The sermons are printed substantially as they were delivered, with a few adjustments and omissions. But some repetitions will inevitably be found in such a series. I have used freely other publications of my own. I have not attempted to indicate indirect quotations and adjusted phrases.

For permission to reprint some of the sermons I have to thank Colonel John Murray, the Northern Newspaper Syndicate, the *Christian World* Pulpit, and Commander Locker Lampson ; and I am very much indebted for help in preparation for the Press to Mr. Robert Stokes and the Rev. R. Hurd.

B. N.

Feast of the Epiphany, 1932

PROLOGUE

I HOPE that the Sermons in this volume may
fairly justify its title ; for, so far as they go, they
refer to English life and the influence of the English
Church upon it.

The first Part speaks of some National aspects of
the English Church, of English Law and Christian
Patriotism. In the second there come into view such
topics as English Education, Christianity and Punishment, English Home Life, our Public Schools, an
English Girl's Religion. In another group of sermons
I go on to speak of Worship in its English surroundings,
of Art, and the Beauty of Holiness.

The third portion deals with Doctrine and Dogma ;
the necessity of their formulation and its inherent
weakness are discussed. The special responsibilities
of English Laymen are indicated, concerning which
the interesting words of Professor Trevelyan will be
remembered :

In England the Church had kept the outline of its ancient
organization, remaining purely clerical in its internal struc-
ture ; it followed that the control of the laity over its
liturgy and doctrine had to be exercised not from within
but from without, through Crown and through Parlia-
ment. . . . In Scotland the laity took an active part in
Church organization and government.

Later I refer to Marriage Ideals, and at the end,
perhaps fittingly, comes a sermon, " Fellowship with
the Departed," which, though preached in memory of
King Edward, has a wider reference. A brief Epilogue
concludes the volume.

It must be said at once that the book makes no
attempt to give an ecclesiastical or doctrinal survey of
the place which the Church of England holds in the

Universal Church of Christ. So far as this volume is concerned, it is enough merely to mention this limitation. It may, however, be worth while to add here in a more general way a few words in this connexion.

A correspondent asked me whether I could meet his perplexities by naming a book in which the position of the Church of England was declared. I explained that I knew no such book, nor did I think that such a book could ever be found, for the reason that the Church of England does not represent a clear-cut system of dogma and practice which must be rigidly and authoritatively enforced. Like Christianity itself, it stands primarily for a life rather than a creed ; its Apostolic Creed is necessary to its life, but the full interpretation of the scope and outlook of the Church of England will be found in the hearts and characters of its own sons and daughters. Its position can be apprehended and recognized, but not defined once for all. The biggest things in the world elude definition and circumscription, but they are not the less clear or real for that.

It is because the Church of England is such a school of character, looking for its exemplar to the primitive discipleship of Christ's first followers, testing its growing thought by Holy Scripture, and believing in the constant guidance of the Holy Spirit in view of fresh situations near home and far off that it is for its children a living spiritual bond of Empire. No scheme of ritual or dead rules could be that. There have been Colossians in every age, and they are with us to-day, who make more of externals than of the devotion of the heart. These in their approach to Christ will substitute the line of outward ordinances for the glow of the eager spirit which rises unfettered to meet its Risen Lord. This is not the way of the English Church, for its aim is so to preach the word of God and administer the sacraments, and so to rear its adherents, that they may bring the mind of Christ to bear upon the ideals and upon the conduct, personal and public, of each generation.

The following paragraph from one of the reports of the Lambeth Conference of 1930 may be quoted in illustration :

And what are these ideals [i.e. of the Anglican Communion] ? They are the ideals of the Church of Christ. Prominent among them are an open Bible, a pastoral Priesthood, a common worship, a standard of conduct consistent with that worship, and a fearless love of truth. Without comparing ourselves with others, we acknowledge thankfully as the fruits of these ideals within our Communion the sanctity of mystics, the learning of scholars, the courage of missionaries, the uprightness of civil administrators, and the devotion of many servants of God in Church and State.

Without pursuing the subject of " Anglicanism," with which this Report is concerned, we may, in a more limited way consider the future of the Church of England, so far as to note some considerations which bear upon it. And in speaking of the Church of England we bear in mind that its oldest part, the Church in Wales, has only recently been severed from it, and that our debt to the Church of Ireland is fundamental.

First, there is a fear lest the special characteristics of our Church should be endangered by its becoming too much the Church of the clergy. These are days when specialization and professional efficiency are extolled. Partly through this tendency, and partly from a particular view of the grace of Orders, there is now a risk that the clergy may become a priestly caste away from the main stream of national and ordinary life, and even away from the religious life of the nation. I have written elsewhere : " It is the general sweetening of the conduct of the community by the Spirit of Christ which counts for most. It would be a disaster if religion in common life and the system of the Church were to become separated in the least degree."

Secondly, we may dread, as a consequence of this clerical professionalism, that the Church may become exclusive in its bearing towards those who have little or no contact with the Churches, and cease to recognize goodness, wherever it is found, as belonging to God, and therefore as coming within the range of the Church's fostering care. We must not let any good people, young or old, resentfully or pathetically think that the Church has no use for them. They must feel at home in church, and with the Church, even if the Church has to educate them in churchmanship. The Church's own welcome must be wider than its own churchmanship.

Thirdly, we have to face the false but prevalent notion that we can have Christianity without Christ, or, rather, that Christianity is unnecessary ; that the ethical excellence of Christian teaching is independent of any personal discipleship of Christ. So long as there are Christians who are true to Christ, their influence will indirectly permeate the general outlook ; and what has been called the " afterglow " of Christian faith and conduct will last on for a while among those who have abandoned Christian belief. But in the long run the good moral effects of Christianity are bound up with belief in the Divine Christ.

In the fourth place, the English Church, like other Churches and agencies for good, is confronted with the secularization and materialism of the time. These are not new forces in the world, but the arrogant self-confidence with which they claim successfully to cover the whole range of human affairs is new. They now assert their dominance as something which leaves no room or reason for any other loyalty. Progress is their prerogative ! When we ask " Progress to what goal ? " their voice becomes less certain. The whole-hearted Christian is on firmer ground ; he knows that the only progress worth having is the progress which leads to God. The only true antidote to this earth-bound materialism is found in the Living Christ. And He does more than cure the baser things of the world : he transfigures them. The English Church brings beauty into barren spots.

Side by side with this outside weight of secularization, we have to reckon with the hesitation of lukewarm believers to make the ventures of Faith. Perhaps this is characteristic of all the life of the age. We dislike responsibility ; we are not independent ; we are so much afraid of our critics. The soldier in the field, so we are told, too often looks for official direction of each step. The author thinks more of the public than of his message. We tremble before newspaper comment, and not only public-spirited, honourable criticism, but even when it is of a manifestly impertinent and superficial kind. We dare not " let ourselves go," to use a popular phrase. Few will stand strong when all is not quite clear. Many wish for some one to lean on or some formula to quote ; they are less anxious to do the right thing, which it may be hard to discover and to do, than to make a plan that will excuse themselves if things go wrong. In what should be a search for the thing that is right, these get no further than the thing that looks safe.

In the fifth place the Church of England has too long, too sacred, too secure a history behind it to be scared by the upheavals of the post-war phases of society. We look upon the War as a temporary episode in the story of the world. It has brought vast changes after it, but the War itself, with its ghastly horrors, belongs to the past. There is no reason why we should consider the present post-war mentality as permanent. It too will have its influence upon that which will follow ; but it will in due course find its level. We can already see the swing of the pendulum in art and in criticism. It need not always be the case that people should look upon every question as " a problem." It is one thing to welcome fresh light from every source, another to regard everything as an open question. In spiritual matters this attitude is against the spirit of the English Church and against the English mind, which is more practical and prefers rather to act on principles than to explore them.

The Archbishop of Armagh (Dr. D'Arcy) has spoken of " the English people, with their profound common sense and their happy disregard of the abstract doctrines of the theorist." The frame of mind which rejoices in " problems " is not too eager for their solution, nor for the duties which it may involve. It stands back and looks at the ways of God with no sense of responsibility, and as if we were in possession of a knowledge which could comprehend the whole as God sees it. It may well be that in the near future the real interest in the Godward side of life which is being shown in many quarters will develop, and the *dilettante* manner will be discarded.

The sermons in this volume deal more fully with some of the points just raised. If they are English in their outlook, they owe much to a happy intercourse with Englishmen, young and old, of different types, and reveal something of what the writer has tried to learn and to teach. The stamp of the greatest of his English masters, Bishop Westcott of Durham, will, he hopes, be found at least in some degree upon them ; and it would be hopeless to attempt to weigh his indebtedness to the great Bishop in thought and sometimes in expression.

It is true that many besides my correspondent *are* inquiring to-day, What does the Church of England stand for ? These pages of course do not pretend to answer the question. I shall indeed be contented if, dealing with truth, beauty, and right character in various settings, they are found to indicate some outlines of our English response to the Love of God in Christ.

PART I
THE CHURCH AND THE NATION

I

THE CHURCH, THE EMPIRE, AND EMIGRATION [1]

" The Lord shall preserve thy going out."—Ps. cxxi. 8

EVERY Englishman may claim the ministrations of the National Church, leaving out the few exceptions of persons who, though English, have adopted a faith hostile to the Church of England. It is a blessed fact that, thanks to our wonderful parochial system, there is no one whom some one clergyman of the Church of England is not privileged to serve. When he is called to exercise his sacred office in one special parish, the Bishop commits to him in solemn words the cure of the souls of the parishioners.

Some of those who live in the parish may prefer the ministrations of some one else, for no one is forced to attend the Parish Church, or to seek a guide in the priest and pastor of his parish. But all who *do* want a friend have one at hand to help them ; and unless a parish priest has a small mind and a smaller heart he will not be eager to draw a sharp distinction among the people whom he may so help. Fortunately, in England, we are not too precise ; and just as those who belong to the Free Churches will still speak of the Parish Church as " our church," and will love to be married in it, and to leave their dearest in the old churchyard, so will the wise parson rejoice to be the clergyman of all. Many of the difficulties in our parishes to-day come from a man appealing to one section of his church people more than to another. His real glory is to unite them all in one, and also to share

[1] A sermon preached on St. George's Day, April 23rd, 1929, in St. Dunstan's in the East, in connexion with the St. George's furtherance of Empire Settlement.

all he possibly can with those who do not in the fullest
sense belong to the Church of England. His sense of
Christian fellowship will overstep his churchmanship.

Now, if the clergy of the Church of England occupy
this position at home, giving to them, as it does, an
opportunity of wider work, a richer field of humble
service than naturally falls to those who serve special
congregations and not whole parishes, similarly the
National Church of England as a whole has a special
influence of its own farther afield across the oceans.
Of course, in the Empire the Church of England holds
no unique position ; yet it cannot be denied that its
vocation in England does make it provide what I
would venture to describe as a spiritual home for the
Christianity of our brothers and sisters in the overseas
dominions of the King. I do not mean that this statement could be justified numerically ; I am rather
speaking of the sentiment of Christian union, and of a
religious focus of Imperial cohesion and concentration.
Sentiment counts for much ; at any rate for much
more than logic, which, among Englishmen, will never
by itself forge a strong link of comradeship.

An illustration of this lies close at hand in these
happy days. If we are asked the question, " What is
it that binds the British Commonwealth of Nations
together ? " we should have to say that there is very
little in the way of ratified agreements, or fixed consti-
tutions and covenants. We could, however, mention
many strands in the strong cord which unites them.
There are our common traditions, a common literature,
a common law. But, in the first place, far beyond all
else comes our one King. The sentiment of love and
loyalty to his throne and person belongs to all his
subjects under whatever skies they live, whatever
language they speak, whatever their colour, whatever
their forms of worship. If this was not apparent
before, it was made clear in the years of the Great
War, and perhaps still more plain in these days of

peace. During our common alarm in every part of the world, the first news sought from day to day was the news of His Majesty's health. It was like a great anxiety in the family. The loving solicitude, watching around the sick-room, has brought us all closer. Our common prayers have linked us together in one close fellowship. We have found, I might almost say, one shrine in which we all have prayed. Some such sense of brotherhood belongs to the devotion of which our National Church is the common centre.

But it is not only in sentimental ways, strong as they are, that it can foster the cause of Empire. To-day we are thinking of Empire Settlement, and here our Church has special responsibilities and opportunities. It is observable that societies grouped round the Parish Church tend to have a greater stability and permanence than others. I suppose this is partly because the Church of England has been bound up with the life of the English people from the beginning. The Church of England possesses a long, long, con-tinuous life. It was one before the Nation became one. The Church and the Nation have been intermingled in their growth. Therefore as soon as an enterprise becomes identified with the Church it is attached to a living, lasting, national body ; pervasive too, so as to be in touch with all. There is a danger in movements which owe everything to one great leader. It is exceedingly difficult to enable them to outlast the dis-appearance of his vivid, urging personality. No plan can secure the perpetuation of the first enthusiasm.

I can see, then, a great advantage in affiliating this great emigration movement, so far as may be, to the Church of England. Such an assertion does not imply that one could wish to disparage or discredit other bodies and other like enterprises : far from it. Thank God there are many which have it at heart. So large a question must be dealt with in large and various and comprehensive ways. All I venture to say is this—

that the Church of England has special powers and opportunities; that it is independent of one passing set of leaders; that again and again it has shown its capacity to renew its strength; therefore it offers a fitting ground in which to plant some of the roots of this world-wide endeavour.

I ought to add that the very parochial organizations in which it flourishes throughout our land endow it on the more practical side with special facilities for this task. The parish priest who, as we have seen, is in touch with all his people can quickly disseminate the needed information among them. In our country districts, at any rate, he knows his people well enough to form a first judgment whether some of them are fit to travel abroad and to become useful members of communities far away. No country is eager to secure the failures from elsewhere. On the other hand, no country is eager to dispatch its most efficient sons and daughters away from the homeland. Some kind of a balance must be struck. In doing this, it is everything to have at hand a man who can detect among the young the promise of satisfactory future development elsewhere, before it has so far ripened at home that they cannot be spared. Here the parochial clergy can exercise their gift of character-knowledge with results that are beneficial to the Empire. One responsible intimate agent everywhere—putting it at its lowest— that is what the Church of England possesses. If this is true of the Church of England in dealing with individuals, it is even more true when we think of the family emigration which constitutes an important aspect of the work. The acquaintance of the parish priest with the families of the parish can be of the utmost service. The members of a small committee must be very skilful and experienced if, in a short interview, they are to come to a right decision about people one by one. It is almost impossible for them to do this in dealing with self-contained families.

They must rely upon the knowledge of those who know the members of the family and the family life as a whole. This is just the knowledge that his intimate association supplies to the clergyman of the Church of England, and he can offer it for the use of those who are in the position of final responsibility.

There is yet one more way in which the Church of England, with others, has a special relation to those who go from England to seek their fortunes in another part of the Empire. It is for the Church at home to build up the characters with which these emigrants will start *as* emigrants. They will begin in their new life by being what they have already become in their old life. If they are not to get on to the wrong track as soon as they land they must already have formed the will to choose and prefer the right. They cannot indeed in England rehearse the life abroad, so far as concerns the details of the problems which will confront them. But, just as a wise emigration policy tries to give, either in England or within the first weeks after arrival, some useful education and preparation for the actual tasks which lie before the emigrants on the other side, so also can the Church of England and every other Church prepare their characters and purposes for the great change. . . .

Lastly, let me point out that the Gospel of Christ abroad is largely judged by the character of those who come from this our Christian country and write themselves down as " Christians " or " Church of England." Christianity is not just a creed ; it is a life. Those who are to be attracted to Christ will be influenced by the lives of professing Christians more than by anything else. One of the greatest setbacks to the spread of Christianity in far-off or heathen lands is to be found in the sight of bad living on the part of those who come from Christian England. It is truly a weighty responsibility for each of us and all of us to bear, that the men and women whom we are constantly meeting are always, consciously or unconsciously, estimating from us the present power of Christ.

*   *   *   *   *

It is for the Church of England to see that those who go abroad shall, by their own bearing, remind others of Christ their Lord, to whom they pledged their love and loyalty in the happy associations of the old parish in England, and in the beloved worship of the old Parish Church.

II

ENGLISH LAW AND UNITY ACROSS THE ATLANTIC [1]

Grant, O Lord, we beseech Thee, that the course of this world may be so peaceably ordered by Thy governance, that Thy Church may joyfully serve Thee in all godly quietness; through Jesus Christ Our Lord.—Collect for Fifth Sunday after Trinity.

THE Collect of the day asks that the course of this world may be so peaceably ordered by God that His Church may joyfully serve Him in all godly quietness. The great profession of the law represented here this morning I believe promotes this grand end in a marked manner.

We hear ignorant people speak as if the law added an irritation to ordinary life which would get on better without it, as if it comprised a mass of technicalities ingeniously devised to benefit the lawyers and to harass other people. In a similar way Christian doctrine is attacked as if it were intended to impose a burden of meaningless formulas to cramp and not to promote the practice of true Christianity.

In reality we find both in law and doctrine the embodiment and the systematization of helpful experience. In growing Church life, after Christ had left the world, men were driven to answer the great questions, " What think ye of Christ ? " " Whose Son is He ? " And they gave their answers in a form which afforded a firm starting-point to others who later, in their turn, were confronted with the same inquiry. But the Apostles' Creed was drawn up by no Council ; it grew and developed as men found through experience of life what were the truths which it helped them

[1] A sermon preached in St. Paul's Cathedral July 20th, 1924, in connexion with the visit of the Canadian and American Bar Associations.

9

most to formulate and to repeat as they ran their Christian course. Doctrine and duty met. You remember Emerson's famous words, "A man's life is the picture book of his Creed." Later creeds, in the face of errors, only made clear what was implicit before.

In a somewhat similar manner law embodies the experience of the past in order to guide the present. There are, no doubt, people who now imagine they can live their own lives, as they say, by cutting themselves off from the past, and in the present by asserting their rights as they estimate them, without respect for the rights of others. These repudiate any restriction and discredit anything that is old and tried, for the mere reason that it *is* old. But wiser men welcome the stabilized experience of previous generations to help them to discharge their duty to the community. Taking pains thoughtfully to revise law and custom as advancing needs require, they are glad to build up the present upon the secure foundations laid in earlier times, and in the same way are they prepared to set out and face the future.

There are several ways in which the recognition of law furthers that peaceable order of this world which we believe to be God's will. First, it has a great negative duty in protecting men from wrong in their relations with others. It preserves us from the fierceness and the fraud of the evilly disposed. There could be no order, no godly quietness, if at every turn men's welfare, their lives and limbs and property, were at the mercy of anyone who chose to attack them. In such a case safe intercourse between man and man would cease, and civilization would sink into savagery. In days long gone by every man defended himself by personal contest ; victory went to the violent. But now law has replaced such an elementary and animal way of settling disputes, for individuals and for societies. It is also, thank God, by a wonderful achievement of our own times, beginning to do something of the same kind in international affairs.

Secondly, law brings liberty—not just the deliverance to which I referred, but liberty, with the ground cleared of hindrances—to develop the best that is in us. In this way does law, enacted and observed, make us free to set forward " peace and happiness, truth and justice, religion and piety," and to prepare the way for the coming among men of the Kingdom of God Whose service is perfect freedom.

Thirdly, laws which are common to those who live under them not only protect them, not only free them, but also unite them through a common bond of trust. Men who can say, " We have the same laws," can say very much more. The law which they share is an outward token of generous fellowship. It tends to bring men's minds together in mutual understanding, so that they grasp one another's point of view because they start from the same background. And it joins their sentiments in an honourable pride to be associated in St. Paul's phrase " as citizens of no mean city," as citizens of a great nation. Moreover, a respect for the laws of one another, when they are worthy of respect, and, better still, an adherence actually to the same laws, so far as that may be—these are potent factors in drawing together a great empire, a great family of nations, and indeed a far-flung federation of nations. Tyranny is a hateful word to the modern world ; but the thing itself may appear under false names and in false dresses, and, of course, legal machinery may be prostituted to press forward a masked tyranny. So was it in the story of Daniel ; so has it often been since his day. But one great antidote against privileged enactments lies in the recognition of Law and Order as a whole—the Law which favours none, the Order which rests upon the goodwill of all. Yet it is not easy for any one country by itself to set up this as an international conception of human life under God's government, if it stand up like one island in the sea with the raging waters of uncontrolled and lawless nations and notions surging round it. But, as more and more related or unrelated nations come to be at one in a fine conception of law and good government, island is added to island in that sea ; yes, and continent to continent ; and then what was perhaps just a firm foothold on the first island develops into broad paths and great roads where men may pass and repass unmolested, helping fellow-wayfarers as they travel upon the King's business—the business of the King of kings—gladly obedient to that Order which is " heaven's first law."

In some respects richer opportunities in this direction lie within reach of Law than of Politics in the limited sense ; the latter vary with the emotions, often with the prejudices of the hour. Law is, by contrast, stable and permanent. It has been said that nothing brings two men more quickly together than close companionship in labouring at some noble task dear to both, where each comes to respect the abilities and the powers of the other ; official joint work leads on to personal admiration and regard. Not different, I believe, is the chance for the lawyers mustered this morning from either side of the Atlantic under the great dome, surmounted by the Cross, which offers consecration to the lives of English-speaking worshippers from near or from far. If they come to know and respect one another as they work at a common task, and welcome in the area of law fresh possibilities of cohesion, rising into view over a wider horizon, a union of hearts may result, grandly extending itself to many others besides themselves, and beyond the borders of their own countries. So would they bring nearer the happy state when

> Heaven breathes through every member of the whole,
> One common blessing, as one common soul.

All those, then, who rightly administer good law are not administering frigid enactments, but providing for human life, individual and social, in a humane way, and may in their place, in some degree, contribute to a world-wide welfare.

But at its best human law only points forward to divine law—the law of God as it was finally proclaimed by the words and the example of our Lord Jesus Christ. Human law carries with it no promise of its fulfilment as the divine law does for those who will have it so, " Walk in the spirit, and *ye shall not*, ye shall not, fulfil the lust of the flesh." Human law cannot really probe the depths of motive and responsibility : witness the present discussion on irresistible impulse in the criminal. But Christ's delicate touch reaches to the very depths of personality.

> Guard my first springs of thought and will,
> And with Thyself my spirit fill.

And Christ *Himself* is near to guide His people, a present Lord, not a memory or a tradition, no ancient or absent law-giver to whom we look back ; He is One Who now speaks in the council chamber of the contrite and humble heart. And the Holy Spirit gives His special grace on each occasion, great or small, to every one who desires—as was said of the last of the Barons of the Exchequer, to every one who desires

> To learn and practise all the law of love.

This law of love is in our Chambers learnt from Christ ; it is practised in the world-wide Courts where He is Judge Supreme.

III

THE CHURCH AND THE LIFE OF ENGLAND [1]

*" Of Him, and through Him, and to Him, are all
things."—Rom. xi. 36.*

BEFORE I begin my sermon this morning I wish
to express my thanks to the Bishop for his gracious
invitation to preach in your Cathedral Church to-day.
I love the memory of my associations with the eastern
half of this Diocese ; nor can I ever forget the welcome
which I received there during the first three years of
my episcopate, which may seem to you to be long ago,
seeing that I have watched the arrival of three successors to myself in that part of the great See of Norwich.
I treasure still the friendships which I then made; I
value the recollection of my visits to Ipswich and of
the last Diocesan Conference there over which I
presided. I gladly recall my visits to the village
churches ; and all is so vivid in my grateful heart that
I can scarcely believe that these things belong to the
years before the War.

" This is an age of progress," it was once said.
" Progress to what ? " was the rejoinder. For change
does not necessarily mean progress. Real progress
must lead to God. Its advance in that direction is its
test.

It is obvious that our generation has seen much
·change and movement in material surroundings. I am
speaking of changes later than the date of the inception
of the protracted process, not yet completed, termed
the " Industrial Revolution," which removed the old
whole-time or half-time village industries, and made
all village life practically to depend upon agriculture

[1] A sermon preached in the Cathedral Church of Bury St. Edmund,
October 2nd, 1927, on the occasion of the meeting of the Church
Congress.

alone. Fresh means of communication have revolutionized the habits of the people. This is the case whether we look far or near. The problems of the world and of our own country are largely due to the way in which the world has grown smaller and the markets of every country, east and west, affect the commerce of almost every other country. Look at the great industry of agriculture, which is of vital concern to us who live in this part of England, and see how in a country, unable to support itself, it is dominated by influences largely beyond our own control. Landlords and farmers and farm-workers as producers, those who dwell in our countryside and in the great centres of population as consumers, alike must bow before facts which call for carefully concerted action both of individuals and of the State. Sometimes we read of the distress in the coal-fields, sometimes of the distress in the corn-fields, and the authorities upon each of these industries, and upon other industries also, seem unaware that they are all together and equally suffering from the same world-wide pressure which is the result of world-wide interdependence.

Nearer home, rapid means of what one may call domestic transport has altered the methods of our people on weekdays and on Sundays. In days gone by most of those who lived in a parish never moved outside its borders. The life of the community was confined within its small circle. Not so to-day. Villages are linked together, and all of them with the neighbouring town. The country town has ceased to be an independent local metropolis, for its residents go far afield for all purposes, and others are constantly coming into it and passing through. Just the same is true of the transmission of news : we hear of what is happening all over England or in foreign lands as soon as it occurs. I need not illustrate the wonders of the telegraph and the wireless.

Glance at Sunday for the moment, and you will find

that its problems, as they are called, largely arise from the improved methods of getting about. Where is the congregation of the village church ? Often outside the village altogether, where their cars and their bicycles have carried them. Where are the Sunday School teachers ? Not absent because they are idling at home, but right away from their homes. Traditional Sunday observance, so we have been told by the Bishop of Durham, has been swept away just by those same facilities which in other directions have made the world so small.

Let me pass to changes of thought. The splendid light of modern science and the development of new views on social problems and relations have brought with them changes which are no less striking. The *Zeitgeist*, as the Germans call it, casts its spell upon us all. No one can remain uninfluenced by the general tendencies of thought around him. And all the more because books are so cheap. Again, the Press is so well organized that a speaker does not now speak to the few who gather to listen to him, but to the tens of thousands reached by the report of his words. The general outlook of men upon one another, of one set of people upon another set, of one class upon another, has all been changing ; and all this intercommunication gives a publicity and a coherence to every set of views which makes them carry the more weight. We can readily see that the new study of history and science has necessarily changed our views of the Bible, so far as concerns its affinities with this world. Fresh knowledge of other civilizations and other literatures must have their bearing upon the historical setting of the Bible. Questions relating to the authorship and compiling of its books, to the manner of the transmission of the texts, and so on, are raised among us which were unknown to our forefathers.

Changes are no less apparent in administration and management. A greater cohesion, mental and material, has unified England and the direction of it in a remarkable degree. Thus, more and more, do things tend to become centralized in London as the capital of the country and Empire. Provincial traditions and feeling are strong, very strong, still ; but they cannot work themselves out apart from the influence and pressure coming from the centre. The War showed us what county feeling can still gloriously do ; but it can only act within that area which a uniform and general attitude of outlook marks out. The War itself, with its paramount demand for one purpose in the nation and in the Empire, set its seal to, and promoted, this tendency to unification, guided from headquarters.

This is clearly seen in the Church. The Church Assembly in London controls what is done in the various dioceses in a way quite unknown when I was first a bishop, while the centralization at Lambeth, which the tendencies that I have mentioned were already bringing about, became instantaneously accentuated in the War. In old days every diocese gave a more individual contribution to the life of the whole Church of England. Now there is a growing sameness among the dioceses. Our finance, too, is comprehensive : there is a central Church Fund in regard to which we all owe a great debt to the capable work of the leading laymen in your diocese.

This centralization has led to an elaboration of machinery and organization in all our public life, and the Church offers no exception. Conferences and committee work, with the careful preparation and publication of excellent reports, have increased beyond all precedent. When I first came to work in this part of the world, I came to the charge of a thousand parishes. Such work could not be attempted by a man who now has to be repeatedly in London for longer and shorter spells, and spends a lamentable amount of time in journeying to and fro for meetings there.

2

It is not irrelevant to note the way in which such new systematization has affected the life of the parish priest. Consider all the new statistics and the returns which he has to make. Think of the growing precision with which he has to meet financial obligations, of the new pension scheme, of fresh arrangements in regard to tithe. These things are beneficial, as we hope, for the whole Church in the long run, though at the moment they are carried through with at least grave inconvenience to many. And recent ideas and the ease of moving about have truly had much influence upon parochial life, not only for the people but for the outlook and the situation of the vicar. It is common to-day to hear people saying that no incumbent ought to remain for more than some ten years in a parish, because of this sense of stir which is in the air. Few of the clergy now seek to live and die in a parish to which they went when they were young. Often I look round upon the monuments in a church and see one and another dedicated to the memory of such-and-such a man, for thirty, forty, fifty years " Rector of this Parish." I recall a window erected to the memory of a man for seventy-five years rector of a Norfolk parish. We shall not see this in the future.

In all these ways, greater or smaller, I repeat, change has come. Is it progress? We are all on the march. In what direction?

The answer rests with ourselves, and with the use which we make of the never-failing grace of God. It is quite possible for us to allow the unquestioned movements of our times to move us from God. It will be our privilege to see that they bring us nearer to Him, to " Jesus Christ, the same yesterday, and to-day, and for ever." " Unto them that look for Him shall He appear." He has something to say to us which He could not say to our ancestors. He has work for us to do which they could not have undertaken.

It is, for instance, possible for us to allow the new

light shed upon the Bible's page to blur its Divine meaning. We may think that its spiritual message has been discredited through altered views of its mundane surroundings. We may think that the unique revelation of God to His chosen people carries less weight because other peoples, so far as the mere words go, have said something which sounds not dissimilar. We may think that the new unions and brotherhoods established among men have rendered the great fellowship in Christ obsolete and unnecessary. We may think that our new schemes of Church finance have replaced the emotions of Christian charity. The teaching of the children on a Sunday about the things of God may seem to belong to a discarded world. Sunday worship itself may appear unnecessary to those who, abandoning apostolic precept, think that they can get more from separately seeking God under the blue dome of heaven in the open country than in assembling together—assembling not so much with the aim of getting something for themselves, as to unite with the whole Christian body in giving to God the tribute of their worship. If these are our thoughts, our change is not progress ; it is only change : " Change and decay in all around I see."

To-day, then, I call myself and I call you to the effort which is necessary to insure that we do make progress towards God, to ensure that every new opportunity of life and thought is used for God. " O Thou who changest not, abide with me." It may be no longer possible to keep the jewels of the old world which is passing from our reach in their old setting. Some of them may even need to be re-cut ; but let us be sure that we do not heedlessly throw them away. It is to such a work of continuance that I devote the remainder of my sermon.

I speak in a country diocese as one who, though he works in a diocese in which more of the population resides in city, borough, and town than in the villages, yet is constantly brought in contact with the life of village and hamlet. And I first emphasize the necessity of maintaining the sweetness and neighbourliness which can still be made a part of country life, in spite of that petty criticism and ill-natured gossip which have always sprung up as weeds among the fair flowers of our garden. Now that the new opportunities give to all the ambition to advance, only too easily does there arise towards those who, in the phrase, seem " better off," a spirit of envy in the hearts of many who are not aware that the position of a true leader does not provide special opportunities of self-enjoyment so much as a heavy weight of responsibility. It has, alas, now come about that some of the persons who live in the bigger homes are unable any longer to share their privileges with those who live in the smaller, because if with a good heart they try to do so they are told that they are acting in a patronizing manner, and patronage is not wanted ; while those who live in the smaller homes do not, on their side, give that priceless present of loving interest in all the family joys and sorrows to those who, differently placed, are yet one with them in the yearnings of the human heart. Let us still all be neighbours. The rich can be selfish ; so can the poor. The poor can be self-centred ; so can the rich. The Old Testament constantly condemns the heartless rich ; it also warns us against unjust judgment in favour of the poor (Lev. xix. 15). Let us all be neighbours, I say. Let us foster those things which draw us together and do not divide classes. Let us not come to look upon one another with a sympathy no greater and a tenderness of feeling no nobler than can be represented by a cash relation. The old life had its obvious and deplorable faults ; yet we must take care that in removing them we do not remove any beauty which it possessed.

So in the modern organization of charity in the limited sense, we must be on our guard that we do still care for the persons whom our schemes are meant to help; that in our central control we are in sympathy and feeling comradeship with the remoter persons with whom we deal. We may come to view our contributions as we view the rates we pay; treasurers of funds often take the delicate bloom off the response of their supporters by sending bald receipts with no charm of personal thanks.

Again, it is a great thing to-day to think of the shorter hours of work enabling young and old to have more leisure. But there is no gain here if the leisure is not kindly, happily, and intelligently employed, or if industry and pride in good work are lost—that sort of pride which led the church-builders of old times to take as much pains over that bit of the carving which would be out of sight as this bit which all can see and admire.

We must to-day be watchful not to lose the spirit of manly independence in facing responsibility which has done much for the building-up of England. People will think they show independence by discarding good manners, by ceasing to be considerate and respectful to those below them or above them in the social scale. I am not thinking of that kind of independence. I mean the independence which enables a man to stand up and to stand alone, if need be, for what he believes to be right; of that independence which leads one in authority not to play for safety or popularity or the avoidance of blame, but to do the right, leaving the issues to God. Too often in our public life a man will refuse to take a proper initiative, lest his act should be exposed to censure or misjudged, lest he should have to bear the loneliness of a grave and a brave decision. Our general levelling up and levelling down may lead to a dead level of going with the crowd; men fear to be or say anything but the average; courage is rare.

Once more, if the best is to prevail in Church or State, we must not worship the machine and think that the perfect organization of which I spoke means perfect work ; it is only an invaluable implement which must be used, and not glorified, if it is to lead to success as God counts success.   It is a great thing to be able to depute to departments the execution of well-considered plans, to have the appropriate committee at hand, the apparatus which is required ; to be able to turn to the expert and hear his pronouncement ; to move with a united front.   But it will be a high price to pay for that greater force which can come to the Church of England from co-ordination if we are to sacrifice the riches of variety and spontaneity.   We must not lose the personal effort, the human sympathy.   Without these things the ablest administration counts for little in the Kingdom of God.   It was through the simplicity and directness of His human appeal that the Lord made an opening for His Divine message.

*   *   *   *   *

It is those that are ready to learn from Christ who possess the secret of real progress ; it is they who bring nearer the great consummation when, in Him, the world shall be brought back, redeemed, purified, sanctified, glorified, brought back to Him " of Whom, and through Whom, and to Whom are all things.   To Whom be glory for ever, Amen."

IV

CHRISTIAN PATRIOTISM [1]

"Let us do good unto all men."—Gal. vi. 10

VIRTUE as a whole, and virtues in particular, represent a mean between extremes. This is a truism, but one of those truisms which need to be protected from misinterpretation. When we speak of a mean we are quick to think of it as a something so carefully balanced as to lose all momentum. But no true virtue is so colourless and vapid, or so much afraid of falling into the dangers which beset it on the one side and the other, as to think that the safest policy is to stand still.

Again, when we speak of virtue as a mean we must not find ourselves supposing that it is the result of correct and nicely adjusted rules. The most casual observer can see that this is not the case, and no one can look at the teaching of Our Lord and His Apostles without seeing that Christian graces are not created by rules. Our Lord's teaching is often in contrast with the fixed methods and regulations for making good Christians, which have been too often adopted by rigid and frigid churchmen of later dates. Christ taught His hearers by large principles, and if we turn to the Sermon on the Mount, which, as we have it, is His most fully elaborated discourse, we see the way in which some rule spoken to them of old time is not so much discarded as interpreted afresh into a larger principle, which displaces the limited prohibition.

We must add that virtue as Christ taught it was not inculcated mainly by bringing even such principles to the minds of men. It was enforced by the illumination

[1] A sermon preached in Westminster Abbey April 22nd, 1928, on behalf of the Royal Society of St. George.

of His own action, disposition, and bearing : " Go and do thou likewise."

We are here to-night to think of the noble but very delicate virtue of Patriotism. Let me at once say that any patriotism which can be offered to God humbly and sincerely, and can be sanctified by His approval, is good and lovely. But perhaps in our own age we have more than ever to remember that patriotism, love of our country, is such a mean between extremes. When methods of communication, improved with startling rapidity, seem to make the world to grow smaller every day, when the impact of nations upon one another is as constant as it is direct, far more difficult does it in consequence become to assign to patriotism its right value and direction than was the case in previous generations. We cannot now regard any nation or group of nations as a self-contained unity. At a time when great peoples linked to one another by close ties of kinsmanship of common traditions, and of united devotion to the Person and the Throne of one Sovereign, are, with all the goodwill in the world, finding it no easy task to adjust the development of their mutual relationships, it is not surprising that in dealing with foreign countries patriotism must be allied with circumspection. We can here quickly recognize the extreme on either hand from which patriotism has to disengage itself. On the one side it is possible to adopt the apparently generous but really ineffective line of " Live and let live." A strictly literal interpretation of these words is the surrender of all effort towards co-operation and mutual service. We must expand such a motto, if it is to be in any sense a worthy international watchword, and say " Live well and help others to live well also." We do not wish to see keen and zealous patriotism move into an inactive cosmopolitanism, for it will vanish in the transition. On the other side patriotism, though it must be ardent and devoted, can take the line of an aggressive self-assertion, interfering, selfish, insolent, so full of itself as to have no contribution to make to the true welfare of other peoples.

Thus, then, we have reached some of those principles which belong to a wise and great-hearted patriotism. It is right to be self-conscious, but wrong when it is wholly self-centred. In many ways we may say that our English patriotism has affinities with the English realization of liberty and the English love of it. Liberty does not mean that every man has a right to do as he pleases, but that every man is free to be at his best and to enjoy his freedom. But anyone who is at his best cannot ignore the rights of others or make little of his privilege to help them too to be at their best. I believe that such an attitude of mind in a nation—and is it not more the attitude of its heart than of its mind ?—will lead a nation to make the most of all that is good at home, and lead it honourably and simply to take its place in the comity of other nations in such a way as to spread a beneficent influence abroad. We have been told that " never in our history have people in other lands looked to us more than they do to-day to give the world an example of world-wide political progress."

But any nation which has this ambition before it will remember that all prevailing influence rests, in the long run, not upon abilities, but upon character. The sadness of our Lord's tears, His patriotic tears, the sadness of His lament, " Oh, Jerusalem, Jerusalem," was provoked by the fact that His dear and native land, with all the wonderful ability of her sons, had failed in the character which its Messianic hope was meant to train in her. The highest patriotism will reveal itself in an earnest effort to build up character, national character, as the sum and crown of personal character.

If we love our country, if we are proud of it, it will be our desire to make it efficient in the world by making ourselves efficient in our own tasks. The lover of his country adds a sense of romance to this task of character building. Do you remember the way in which—in perhaps the finest speech recorded in history, outside the pages of the Bible—the great statesman uses the terms of sentimental endearment to express the fervour, the passion, with which the patriotic citizen regards his own land. A lover sees the best, hopes the best ; a lover is tender, self-forgetful, devoted. So will be the patriot towards his country. May I say two things of this devotion ?

It will not become less faithful because it also looks outwards and desires to share with others what it has learnt to prize at home. We have all observed that in the best natures a great love influences and sweetens the general outlook of a man or woman towards the world ; and it does not itself become less deep when it is a fount from which others draw. We do not forget the splendid openness with which the orator to whom I have alluded characterized the welcome offered to all who cared to visit the great city of his countrymen, to drink in, if they could, something of the spirit which had made her so great, her citizens so proud. Never- theless, I suppose that his remarkable phrase, uttered in the circumstances of the times, must have regarded the lover's jealous satisfaction rather than his expand- ing power of affection. But Christ has come since then, and from Him both individuals and nations have learnt lessons which the Athenian could not know. He has taught all persons and peoples that their gifts are trusts ; "nothing is our own except our opportunities, and over these is written, ' Occupy till I come.' " It is this sense of responsibility to God which will prevent our forgetting in unreflecting patriotism, and our misusing what we rightly call the Mission of the British Race. Our Empire is a fact of history, but it is a force as well as a fact. Yet only those whose hearts and imagina- tions are touched by God will be fully competent to direct that gracious force aright and to lead their white-hot patriotism to accomplish God's purposes. It was largely their self-regarding exclusiveness which long ago stood in the way of the Jewish race bringing to bear upon the world at large the uplifting influences of which their genius for religion had made it capable. But though, if read as mere history, the Old Testament is one of the saddest and most pathetic books in the world, the true Israel was summed up in Christ, to whom the Old Testament pointed forward, the Son of David, the Son of man, with His universal appeal, gathering all nations to Himself, in Himself, into the great Brotherhood before God, the Father of them all.

My second remark is that a devoted love of country should draw out the best contribution that each has to make—the highest, the lowliest—to his Nation's good. Public opinion and personal life are the powers which make and unmake countries. Every one consciously or unconsciously adds his drop to the stream of public opinion. If the drops are clean and clear it will be a crystal river ; but tainted drops will taint the whole. And as for personal life, this counts for much more than is reckoned to-day. We find people more ready to reform the world around them than to reform themselves. Some seem to claim, as a reward for their ardour in criticizing the general order which has been worked out by long experience, a complete freedom for themselves, to live without restraint or any wholesome self-criticism. Anyone who, even superficially sur- veys the habits of our times, will be struck with the zealous demand and excellent effort for public improve- ments, but not less by the absence of disciplined, dedicated lives in too many directions. But our lover of his country will not make this mistake. In his desire to ameliorate the institutions and the methods of the nation, the general direction of its public and social affairs, he will bear in mind that it is what a man or a woman is that gives the quality to their words and their works. " Never mind about yourself, you have to think of others " ; so we are told to-day. " Do not worry about your sins." " Do not trouble about saving your own soul, for that is a very petty and a very selfish concern." This is truth ; but it is half-truth for those who read the whole of the New Testament. At any rate, if, with the standard of Christ in view, His example of personal goodness, humility, and love of God, we were to attempt through the power of the Spirit to respond, each in his place, to his own high calling, we should be doing something very real to liberate our country from everything that is a check to the fulfilment of the dreams of the loftiest and most loving patriotism centred in our own England ; and we should brighten our eyes to gain a clearer vision of its Empire-wide, its world-wide, power for good and for God. The fire of our patriotism must be worthy to be a beacon-light.

V

THE ENGLISH CHURCH: THE DOUBLE TRADITION OF EAST ANGLIA [1]

" The vision is yet for the appointed time : though it tarry, wait for it ; because it will surely come."—Hab. ii. 3

HE would be a bold man who attempted in one short sermon to survey the links which bind this festival to those days of long ago that fill our thankful minds. And indeed we must not to-day too far surrender ourselves to the arresting spell of the past. It is still more important to listen to the call of the future, and see to it that the jewel handed down through the centuries is passed on to those who follow us, reset to reflect a fresh glory of God for the days to come. " A fresh glory," I say, for we cannot repeat the past. What is true of individuals is true of successive generations. Do you remember the striking passage in which Lord Balfour, speaking of the special apprehension of reality granted to each person, prettily compares the way in which we all say we see one pathway of light formed by the sun on the water, when, as a matter of fact, to the eyes of no two persons do the drops throw up exactly the same reflection.

We do not ask to see things as our predecessors saw them. Yet every age may look up into the face of Christ to find that *He* is the " Contemporary of every generation," and that still the true life of man is the vision of God, as seen again and yet again in the face of Jesus Christ. *Vita hominis visio Dei*. Our highest hope must be that a compelling vision may either be given to ourselves or that we may prepare its way for others. This is certainly true in the changed outlook

[1] A sermon preached in the Cathedral Church of Norwich August 13th, 1930, on the occasion of the celebration of the Thirteen-Hundredth Anniversary of the foundation of the East Anglian See.

of which I speak, much changed indeed since the day, when our city was perhaps the second town in England ; and how much more changed since the first years of the great East Anglian See. And with this great hope in view I suggest that in these days when with Job we may say war and changes are against us, in the actual situation before us now, the Church must inspire and consecrate all personal and public life with a fresh breeze from heaven in order that we may attend upon God. The Church must convincingly interpret the call of God in a manner adapted to the circumstances of the hour. No new gospel is asked for, but the old gospel preached to all, for life, and not for argument ; in the language each understands, not in obsolete phrases. *Non nova, sed nove.*

The development of the external organization of the Church is wonderful. Contrast the number of bishops who attended the first Lambeth Conference and the number who have sat under the splendid leadership of him whom we respectfully receive to-day. And here let me say how eagerly in the name of this ancient diocese, we welcome the bishops from far and near who are graciously joining with us in our thanksgiving through word and will, of which our own Bishop Reynolds is the great interpreter. The presence of these biships must set even the least imaginative thinking of the far-flung activity of the Church of Christ, from those old days which the Archbishop of Wales, whom we are proud to honour, represents, up to the foundation of the newest diocese.

But organization does not of itself bring life, nor do conventional Church ways of thought and conduct, nor methods of efficiency learnt from the world. It is possible to be full of movement without real advance. Again, while we are thankful that the spirit of compassionate interest in the welfare of others is abroad, we know that this is not necessarily Christian in its life or outlook, although those who do not name the name of

Christ have often indirectly, and in spite of themselves, derived their finest ideals from Him and His disciples.

The Church must, if I may say so reverently, bring God Himself into our midst, to be acknowledged, relied on, loved, followed, obeyed. That is the secret of progress, the only real advance.

It has been said that the greatness of an age depends on the greatness of its conception of God. How do we stand that test ? Too often I fear those who do think of God will speak as if He existed either to create or to solve problems—to use the favourite word—in their self-limited lives. They do not contemplate Him as He is, or rather as we can know Him, with awe and worship. They do not know Him as supreme and yet their best friend. And there is another test found in our attitude to our fellow-men ; too many will interest themselves in the lowest to which human nature can fall, instead of admiring the highest to which it can rise.

Perhaps these remarks are rightly made in one of the dioceses in which two strands of English Christianity were happily united. Leaving aside the Christianity which reached our shores from Gaul during the Roman occupation, I am thinking first of the vigour of Celtic Christianity when once its torch was lit. " Under it grew a Church, loose in government, but instinct with personal holiness." The Irish Church—what joy to have the Primate and Bishops of the Church of Ireland among us !—" The Irish Church reared saints and missionaries." These carried the Gospel eastward to the north of Great Britain and southward to East Anglia in the seventh century. We do not forget the Irish St. Fursey to-day. We cannot let the gladness and the glow of love for Christ cool down into external rules, however excellent, in which He Himself is drawn from our adoring sight. If the living Christ goes, all goes. On the other hand, clear before us rises the figure of St. Felix, representing the coherent scheme of the Christianity which came to us direct from Rome and

Canterbury.   Both types met in East Anglia.   We can never dare to omit the saintliness from our Christian life ; if we did, it would lose its savour before God and its attractiveness in the eyes of men.   But we require our St. Felix if the Church of Christ is to go beyond its pioneer stage and to hold fast together.   There must be some Church order. Temperaments, however, vary ; and some will always make more of the one saint than the other.

Now, if there is anything to lead us to suppose that at the moment St. Felix is bigger among us than St. Fursey ; if anywhere personal Christianity comes from external direction more than from a spontaneous life that is hid with Christ in God ; if efficiency ever displaces love ; if some of us, with our many engagements, are more busy about the work of Christ than calmly desiring Him to work through us—then on this festival day we may be encouraged to make a fresh start by the Founder of our Cathedral Church, who built it some five hundred years after the date which, as a diocese, we are commemorating.

You are familiar with history.   Our Cathedral, you know, in its strength and in its grace, stands as the beautiful monument of a great penitence.   In the battle of life he came out with scars ; but his contrition made them to be glorious scars of victory won through Christ. The gentleness of unsullied innocence and the power of deliberate repentance are both precious to God.

Our founder reminds us that we are not bound by our past, that lost ground can be recovered, that it is good to try again.   " The sense of failure felt to be failure is the promise of future success."   And the influence of one man here and one woman there who turn again to Christ, with simplicity and renewal of purpose, reaches far.

In the Old Testament it was the Remnant (reduced, it is true) but pure and chastened, faithfully waiting for Him in Whom the hopes of Israel were gathered up and finally fulfilled, which kept bright the vision of God. The New Testament reveals the power of the constant few. These are the leaders who, with their upward gaze, in the end are the saviours of mankind.

There have always been those who are confident of the failure of Christianity. Bishop Butler's words will spring to your mind. But these prophets, whether downcast or bitter, have again and again proved wrong. " They that wait upon the Lord shall renew their strength." Only let us be sure that we are waiting upon Him, watching at midnight or at the cock crowing or in the morning for Christ's call, equipped for Him to use us when He requires us, and then " Unto them that look for Him shall He appear "—perhaps suddenly.

" Perhaps suddenly " : I repeat these words because I believe they are words to encourage us to go on at home and abroad with our work for Christ expectantly. The world about us shows that the usual course of nature is regular and slow ; yet where all has gone undisturbed for centuries a swift and sudden cataclysm may occur. It is so in history also. Only recently a famous scholar defended the view that the outstanding men have a genius of their own and are not thrown up by their times. They *do* change through their own force, suddenly appearing, the cycle of events.

God's ways are commonly slow ; yet at times a goal is reached, and then He will move rapidly. After centuries of preparation it was suddenly that the fullness of the time came, and the angels' song over the fields of Bethlehem heralded a new life for men. Such too was the thrill of Pentecost. So now God may have some purpose to fulfil for our generation or its successor. It is for us to go on sowing, sure that God will bring the harvest in His own way. " God asks for our work not for the issues of it ; they are in His hands." The harvest in East Anglia in a fine summer is an annual surprise of beauty. If we sow steadily, some such surprise of beauty God may have in store for us, in a startling and swift extension of His Kingdom.

Some such thoughts as these stirred in my mind when recently I was visiting Mohammedan lands. To the outward eye the Moslem religion, to give it as an example, seems entrenched, contented. But those very lands before now have seen the unmistakable work of God in providing a sudden redemption. Then why not again? It might come either by some quick outward change of which we cannot now imagine the details, as it did more than once in those old days, or after an inward illumination, opening the eyes of many at the same time to see that secular and material hopes are not enough for the soul of man which was made for God.

*   *   *   *   *

There is no pathway of life at home or abroad until God leads and lightens the way. But if men, by whatever path, do come strongly to grasp the idea that they need, for now and for the Beyond, this vision of God, He will not be slow to reveal Himself to them in His Son, openly, decisively, victoriously.

The word "Gospel" means good news. But in Greek it first means the reward of one who brings good news. That reward will belong to all who by holiness of life, by concentrated effort, by insight and imagination, by the very zeal of waiting, have prepared the way for this Coming of the Lord.

We cannot tell; we cannot prophesy. But the mere hope of the possibility of so great a thing is enough to send us back more eager to our three glad but difficult tasks—prayer, service, expectation, neither cast down by failure nor wearied by the tarrying, with the faith held fast that in God's good time the Vision will surely come.

VI

THE CHURCH AT HOME AND OVERSEAS [1]

" The Word was made flesh."—St. John i. 14.

IT is plainly no use for me to try to expound the volumes carefully prepared by experts and presented at St. Paul's-tide last January. It will rather be my aim to go far beyond the Report, and to ask you to consider with me the way in which the Incarnation, the Death, and the Ascension of the Lord have supplied us, not only with the Message which we preach, but with the assurance of its welcome and its success. In a word, our Gospel has a supreme appropriateness for all who hear it.

And where and when could we consider this great subject more appropriately ? We meet in our grand Cathedral, where the saints of God have worshipped for eight hundred years, and appealed to the Heavenly Father, theirs and ours, and where in their generations men have been raised up to be pillars of the Church, confronting the opportunities and difficulties of their times ; not our difficulties or our opportunities, but all of them serving God in worship and in the use of His gifts, and, in response to His calls, all of them our fellow-disciples.

And we are in the octave of Whit-Sunday, the festival of a great Coming, when for the work of carrying the Gospel all over the world the Church was endued with power from on high. The Lord had not told His disciples how the Holy Spirit would come, only that He would come and replace His personal Presence ; and they were able to abide patiently in Jerusalem, with no sense of loneliness for His absence,

[1] A sermon preached in the Cathedral Church of Norwich May 26th, 1926, on the occasion of the Diocesan Missionary Festival.

only, in a spirit of great expectation, praising and blessing God, till the holy endowment should be given them to equip them for their new work I confess the Proper Preface for Whit-Sunday always appeals to me when it throws us back to that first manifestation of the Holy Spirit, whatever its exact form may have been, and also classes us with the heathen, and reminds us that Britain too needed to be brought out of darkness and error into the clear light and true knowledge of God.

This ought to raise in our hearts a sense of sympathy with the heathen of to-day, who now *are* where our ancestors *were* centuries ago. We are thankful that our country is a Christian country, and we have had fine signs of that lately. But if we are a Christian country it is because, and only because, the Gospel of Christ reached our shores. Christianity was planted among us, and that plant has bloomed and flourished.

I am very proud to think that as I look back through our long line of bishops I stand in the succession from a missionary bishop, happy by name and happy in the work which he and another initiated in East Anglia. I love to look at the reproduction in my house of what not altogether fancifully I may regard to be his portrait.

Before, however, I approach my main theme, I have to make one or two more general observations relating to ourselves at home. First, let us be on our guard that we do not concentrate the call entirely upon this year. There is no doubt no intention to do so ; but, human nature being what it is, it is difficult to keep the flame burning brightly if all attention is given to starting the fire. The World Call is always with us, and has been ever since the day when the Lord first sent the Apostles out to preach the glad tidings and endowed them with gifts for their work.

Again, in this Diocese, this World Call brings up before us the question of the union of benefices. I know, perhaps better than anyone, the sentiments, some right and some selfish, which lead almost every parish, even if it contains only a few hundred inhabitants, to claim to have its own parson, conducting full services in his one church, and confining his ministrations to his one flock, often with a starvation stipend. Yet when one reads of the appalling need of more men even to keep going, without expansion, the work of Foreign Missions, it seems impossible for any man who is placed in a position of responsibility and possesses any breadth of view to come to the conclusion that the parochial outlook is in all cases to be adopted. Are we not bound, in the light of this Call, to show a spiritual wisdom in the distribution of our limited forces ?

Once more, we must not lose the message that comes to ourselves from abroad ; for there are two clear calls addressed to us from the mission-fields afar. The first call is the call for unity. We are asked to set aside our differences at home, " our pettiness and our controversy." Abroad, for example among the Chinese, there is a desire to welcome one Church, and not miscellaneous societies of churchmen and Christians who cannot work satisfactorily with one another. Differences that may be intelligible to us at home, as we contemplate the development of Church history from early days, can and should make no appeal to those who want simply the Gospel of Jesus Christ and Him crucified. It would be a great thing if men with discrepant views at home could keep silence for the sake of the heathen abroad.

The other great lesson which we at home receive from the mission-field is that of the power of God unto salvation.

The love of the sincere converted heathen can make our own hearts to glow again with the light reflected back from them to us. To them Christ is without doubt all in all when they truly accept the appeal of His Name. With us that Gospel has become so

interwoven with other strands of our life without
consecrating them that we do not welcome it with the
eager, glowing zeal with which, for example, it touched
the heart of St. Paul long ago, or now it touches the
hearts of many who know, with a wonderful joy and
gratitude, that it has called them out of darkness into
a marvellous light. They acclaim the Lord with
fresh personal loyalty and enthusiasm who through
death hath destroyed him that had the power of
death, that is, the Devil, and delivered them who,
through fear of death, were all their lifetime subject
to bondage.

I may turn, then, now to my theme ; I want to
make it clear to you that it is the very character and
human nature of Christ Our Lord which makes Him,
if I may say so, able to save the world. I may introduce my subject by a personal reminiscence, venturing
to tell you how the universality of Christ's character
first came to grip me when I was a young man, and
why it has held me ever since.

I often remember those blest and happy days which
I spent with Bishop Westcott before I entered Holy
Orders. He was then new to his position as Bishop
of Durham and had not yet established in his house
that college of young men whom he called his " sons,"
nor would his new duties allow him to enter upon a
regular course of study with me. I was there in fact
in the character of guest rather than in that of pupil.
But, for all that, it was almost impossible for anyone
who was admitted as a friend to that great man's
most casual conversation not to carry away from it
something of more serious value. You entered his
house his friend, you left it his disciple ; so it came
that I would study at my pleasure either in his palace
or in the little lodging pleasantly situated by the sea
to which we retired for a brief change. It was not
his object to cram the mind with already digested
knowledge ; rather would he impart to you his own

zeal and enthusiasm, and his pupil would feel his eyes raised from earth to Heaven and would learn from the Bishop things on which he might have concentrated too narrow an attention in grander and more sublime proportions.

Well do I remember those readings we had together, those explanations he would give of any difficulties I had found in the New Testament, which often enriched me with some finer conception which I could afterwards treasure in my mind and ponder for myself. Particularly do I recall how he promised that towards the end of my time with him he would give me a passage the careful reading of which was to set the coping-stone on his teaching. Before I left him he set me the task of writing a short note on the words of St. John, " The Word was made flesh." My youthful inexperience could find nothing more in it than a statement of the true and entire humanity of Our Lord. At the foot of my sheet, however, he added the following comment : " All that you say is undoubtedly true ; but whereas the word ' $\mathring{a}\nu\theta\rho\omega\pi\sigma$ ' denotes an individual of the human race, the word ' $\sigma\acute{a}\rho\xi$ ' represents the race as such ; Our Lord, as man, united in His Person all those various qualities that are scattered over the whole body of men in all ages and places ; He is the centre, the focus where all meet. See the Epistle to the Galatians (iii. 28), the word ' $\epsilon\mathring{i}s$,' and Goldwin Smith's remarks on the character of Our Lord." It was this that he was reserving till the last. These remarks I will quote.

Now, before we examine this statement a little more fully, I would invite you, as we go, to point the moral for yourselves without my doing so, and to see the appeal that is made to every nation under the sun in the fact that Our Lord's human nature, as shown in His human life, was not circumscribed like our own, but was unlimited in its universality, its comprehensiveness, and its inclusiveness. I would ask you to observe how He gathers up into Himself the different qualities of human nature as they are shown all over the world, and therefore can give of His very own sympathy to meet, of His Power to touch, and of His understanding love to heal, the needs of all what in His human life He was and what He is now as the Son of Man, He is for us all. His finished work potentially includes all the sons of men. He is their great representative, and all the while He is God.

He comprises in Himself all the qualities that are found scattered over the whole number of men. Jesus was man, but, even setting aside all considerations of His divinity, He was more than a mere individual man. Nothing proper to man, as created, but is presented in Him. He is the example of every man and of the whole of man. To force this point home we will return to the lectures on history of Goldwin Smith mentioned above. The point is brilliantly expounded there, and we may almost reproduce his actual words.

The virtues of the human race, as we see them, appear scattered over different individuals ; in Jesus they appear combined. Some are masculine, some feminine. But manly strength and womanly sweetness are both attributes of mankind, so both appear in the character of Jesus, Who thus includes the two sections of the race in Himself. Again, different virtues flourish at different times, and in ethics each age contributes in some respect to advance and beautify the human ideal. Jesus transcends the ideal of any single age. Different countries and different races seem better fitted to practise different virtues. There is a great difference here between the peoples of Europe and Asia. But all good, whether sprung from east or from west, or from any other quarter, appears in nobler form in Jesus. Good men, as a rule, make a stronger claim either to our admiration or to our love.

But who, however closely he scan the pattern of Jesus' life, can say whether it demands our love or our admiration the more ?

Our Lord Jesus is free from all extremes in either direction—a fact which must appear marvellous, nay, rather divinely supernatural, if we think what the world was like in His day. The Jews, impatient of the Roman yoke, would have thought that they were betraying their past traditions and their future hopes had they not resorted to arms or some sort of resistance, in the hope of restoring the Kingdom of God, as they conceived it. But Jesus, with all His faithfulness to God combining a truer view of His Kingdom, bade them " render unto Cæsar the things which are Cæsar's and to God the things which are God's." He would not make Himself their champion, would not claim, in a restricted sense, for His own anything that could not belong to the whole race. He loved His country well and, " seeing the city, He wept over it." His were the words " salvation is of the Jews," and in Jerusalem he recognized the centre of God's purposes in the past. But, for all that, He could say, " The hour cometh, when neither in this mountain, nor in Jerusalem, shall ye worship the Father, but the hour cometh, and now is, when the true worshippers shall worship the Father in spirit and in truth." He did not claim God as the special God of the Jews ; He declared Him to be the Father of the whole race of men and of every individual member of it. Indifferent as he was to the particular aspirations of the Jews, He was equally free from anything that distinguished the Greeks or Romans from men in general. There was nothing in Him to bind Him to any one land, no touch of vice or virtue to divorce Him from the whole race. He lived, indeed, as any other member of His native land ; He was man, and employed the customs, the language, the dress of His country. But in His character, His mind, and His life we find nothing that is not universal. The life of Christ transcends any dissimilarity or distinction of race.

The same is true of those differences that divide the adherents of a system or a school ; what is true is His, what is not true is not His, nor did He establish any rule that is not fit for all men in all places to follow. Bold would he be that should say that any part of Jesus' teaching is discordant or out of date. Living among Pharisees, Sadducees, and other factions, He never inclined to any of them ; nor, more wonderful still, did He ever recoil from any of them to the opposite extreme. Moreover, He has none of those seeming virtues which only suit one time or one race ; such virtues, where they are found, are indeed accounted virtues, inasmuch as their removal would lead to a general deterioration, but their use and value is merely occasional, and had Jesus been distinguished by such His human nature must have suffered in universality.

Lastly, there is nothing of excess or deficiency in Jesus, nothing too that stands out pre-eminent in His life or nature. Such a pre-eminence of any single virtue depends either on its own success or on its presence in the absence of others. The example of Jesus' human nature, then, will never grow faint or die, and there is no possible substitute for it. His human nature is human in a universal sense ; every ethical quality that men require in any time or in any race appeared, once and for all, in the Son of Man when He dwelt with men. This is the sense of His own words, " When the comforter is come, He will convict the world in respect of righteousness, because I go to the Father, and ye behold Me no more." In Him was the absolute, the perfect picture of righteousness in its fullest sense ; and when the world seeks a different or a changed example, it is at once thereby convicted. He is perfect on every side. Never will there be a man who has any other duty than to follow His example from afar.

The words so constantly on the lips of St. Paul—" in Christ Jesus "—draw from this their source and life. " If He were only an individual man He could not gather all men unto Himself : the phrase ' in Christ ' . . . the historic expression of justification by faith, would have no meaning." Jesus, though true man, was not a mere man, not one in the crowd : He *was* man, in whom the whole race could be, so to speak, summed up.

All these glorious lessons vanish from us, I may say, if Jesus Christ is nothing but a mere individual man, " simply one prophet more, greater indeed and more fully inspired, but as one of the prophets," yet not unique—a man, not the " Son of Man."

To the same purpose wrote the Bishop in a brilliant passage : " Seeing that He unites in Himself all that is truly manly and truly womanly, stripped of all the accidental forms, which belong to some one country or to some one period, every one can therefore find in Him for His own work union with the eternal ": " for His own *work* "—shall we this morning rather say, for His own *life* union with the eternal ?

Jesus Christ is therefore the one and the all-sufficient hope of the world ; and those who see Him as He is, recognize in Him an adequate Saviour. He is a saviour indeed for this world and the world to come, as is immediately recognized when once our missionaries have put all that He is and all that He is able to do before the eyes of their converts. And as for the token of their commission from Him, is it not manifest in their own love for these wandering children of God. Love speaks a language which all men can understand without translation. Some of these children of God may have civilizations far, far older than our own ; some may have intellects and minds from which we may learn much. But if they have not the mind of Christ they are only men having no hope, without God in the world. When we pass from the men of learning and civilization of whatever degree to the miserable, ignorant, downtrodden, degraded, and suffering, if all that we have been saying is true, what joy for them to hear from us, that the Lord Jesus has suffered as they have suffered, that He knows from the inside what is meant by pain and persecution : what joy for them to come for relief for all their sickness and agonies of body to the Christian doctor and the Christian nurse whom He has sent forth in His Name to continue His blessed healing work. Except for sin He has known every phase of human life. No one is outside the range of His sympathy. " Unto them that look for Him shall He appear " ; and may He truly appear to our blinded sight at home, to all who open their gaze to see Him as the missionaries proclaim Him abroad—the Friend, the Saviour, the Master, the King, the Son of Man, the Son of God.

It is always a delight to me to use in my intercessions from time to time the pages of our Diocesan Calendar which the Dean will read out to us, comprising the names of our representatives in the Foreign Field, just as it is always a happiness to me to know the number of the young men who offer themselves for ordination from this Diocese. Oh, may the number of both be constantly increased and magnified this year ! and not only in the enthusiasm of this year, but in the years to come. Let nothing keep the young men and young women from offering for service abroad. May many rise up to augment and replenish the list of workers in the Mission Field in which the most varied aptitudes are welcomed !

Passing deeper than the necessary distinctions in the home and the Foreign Field, let me close my sermon by emphasizing yet once again that we are all one, whatever our nation, tribe, capacity, language, colour, civilization, or position ; we are all one man, one in Christ Jesus, Who, Himself Man and God, has through His all-inclusive human nature redeemed us by the blood of His Cross, and in His Ascension as the Head of the human race has presented us before the throne of God. This on His side ; on ours it is for you and me, for our brethren at home, for our brethren over there, to carry in every direction the story of His great love.

VII

THE KING AND THE CHURCH [1]

"Every family." "The whole family."—Ephes. iii. 15.

THE English people are a home-loving people. It is said that their word "home" can be translated into no second language. Certainly they are not a stay-at-home people; they have spread throughout the world. But as they have spread abroad they have carried the word "home" with them across the seas; and the tenderest word which comes to the minds of our distant brothers and sisters as they look back to the England from which they have sprung is still the word "home." It is only to say the same thing in another way to remark that family life is very dear to us.

I do not deny that there is much which tells against home life to-day. I need only mention two among the many of such disruptive forces, the one coming from within, the other from without. The new freedom of the War-time, the impossibility of maintaining the family life at a time when the various members of all families were rendering different kinds of service in different places and manners, led to a loosening of home ties. As a result came that spirit of liberty or licence which tempts people to consider that family obligations may be held lightly, and that the members of one family may look for employment, friendship, amusement, and interest outside the home to such an extent as to cheapen home life altogether. In this manner, all too easily, do homes become degraded into residences. Every civilized language possesses a word meaning "house." Of course this tendency to independence has its good side. The women and girls of

[1] A sermon preached in the Cathedral Church of Norwich July 7th, 1929, at the service of Thanksgiving for the recovery of His Majesty the King.

our own country who nobly responded to the call for patriotic service during the War-time were not likely to content themselves with a return to a dull and ineffective routine. So many of the men were absent for the purposes of the War, that the women had to fill their places; and now many of them still prefer to be up and doing, and many of the girls of leisure of the old days are now compelled to find their own livelihood. All honour to the women and girls for their enterprise and industry. Such independence, then, both when it is worthy of praise and when it is not, has to no small extent altered the traditions of family life.

The second force telling against it to which I allude is the enormously increased facility of transport. People who can so easily travel from one place to another for their work and their recreation are not so likely to remain anchored in one spot, even if it bears the sacred name of home. This aspect of the subject, however, is so plain to see that I need say no more about it.

How far such tendencies, already weakening home life, may proceed I do not prophesy. It is probable that already there is some exaggeration in our estimate of the extent of any decay now found in home life in England. The newspapers to-day are cheaper and far more numerous. Consequently they reach more people, and naturally they record the unusual happenings more than the usual; though I may say, in passing, that I believe that, if we knew all, we should frequently have to praise the self-denying reserve of the Press in not publishing all the sensational matter which reaches its offices. But there is a risk that when we read of the unusual we may persuade ourselves that it is the usual. For example, we may read of smart hostesses who vie with one another in the elegance and luxury of their entertainments; this must not make us forget the quiet, happy intercourse

of hospitality between family groups. Or we may
read of the number of marriages which are dissolved
in the divorce court ; this must not make us suppose
that all married life is being spoilt by such scandals
as those of which we hear. The glory of pure homes
filled with joy and peace naturally is not constantly
being brought before our eyes. Their deep and sweet
contentment invites no flashlight upon its quiet
privacy.

However, on a wide survey, discounting the points
that may inaccurately be urged to the contrary, and in
spite of all that really tells in the opposite direction, I
do not hesitate to repeat my assertion that English
people are by tradition, and are still by temperament,
domestic in their habits and their happiness.

Now, it is plain that all this grace and glory of home
life owes much to Our Lord. Quite obviously family
affection is independent of His teaching. We find
arresting and delightful illustrations of it among the
birds and the animals. It was, of course, to be found
in the old pagan world before Christ came. We have
a touching letter written by the great Roman orator
and statesman on the death of his daughter, and a letter
of sympathy from his friend, though we, who soothe
our family sorrows by the hope that we find in Christ
Who is risen from the dead and become the first fruits
of them that slept, may think that the poor man must
have found it jejune comfort to be invited to consider
the decay of the beautiful towns of Greece, which
brought into view a misfortune on a larger scale than
the death of this one beloved woman.

Again, we may dwell on the persistent strength of
family life among the Jews from the beginning before
Christ came. In Old Testament days, and indeed up
to and in our own times, the Jewish people have set an
example to the world of strong family union, religion,
and affection.

But here, as elsewhere, Christ has taken of the

existing bread and wine of Life and sanctified them by His favour. He has made what was beautiful before more beautiful by His touch. We love to think what it must have meant at the time, and what it means for us still, that He found so much of simple joy and help in the quiet home at Bethany; that He wrought His first miracle in a family circle when two young people were setting out to found a new home of their own; that immediately after a discussion on divorce He took into His arms the little children, who were the offspring of happy marriages and blessed them. It is an ever-lasting consecration of family life and its foundation that in Holy Scripture the Church is represented as the Bride of Christ whom He loves and for whom He gave Himself, that He might present it to Himself a glorious Church, not having spot or wrinkle or any such thing— free, that is, from every stain of pollution and every sign of decay—for Christ's Bride must be holy and without blemish. The marriage of the Lamb uplifts the conception of human marriage; the blessing of Him Who was born into a humble home rests upon every home where He is welcomed.

It was very natural then that the great Apostle should, in his letters, quickly turn to the duties of husbands and wives, and children and servants, after he had illuminated the highest realities in the heavenly places. Christ and His disciples have adorned home life, and have added a new fragrance to this home life which we love. They have also removed, or tried to remove, the things that in the old world degraded human affections.

If then, my friends, this love and life richly blessed and exalted by Christ Himself is truly characteristic of our own race, it will not surprise us to observe that it is a family tie which holds together our British Commonwealth of Nations. Our British Empire is a family. The tie which binds us in one does not owe very much to legal enactments or to official covenants.

4

The constituent elements of the Empire are singularly free to develop themselves along the lines that they may choose. They are not an unrelated body of States bound to one another by formal agreements ; they are sisters in one family. As in ordinary life brothers and sisters are near and dear to one another, just because they are brothers and sisters, so it is in the British Empire. It is the strong bond of family sentiment which holds them. The War proved this, if we had not known it before.

It is therefore no exaggeration to say that to-day we are gathered for a family festival thanksgiving. Family Prayer in the literal sense—that kind of family prayer that the great soldier Lord Roberts made a grand effort to reawaken in England—has, alas, largely fallen into disuse. But at least we still understand the phrase " family prayer " if few are acquainted with the thing. And I may claim to say that to-day we approach the Throne of Grace in one family devotion through the length and breadth of the Empire.

Not only does our Sovereign Lord and King stand at the head of his vast dominions at home and abroad, but, as we thankfully know, this touching world-wide family sentiment meets in him. I am not sure that in his engaging simplicity and humility he himself was aware before his illness and recovery of the depth and tenderness of the loyalty of his subjects. Do you remember the words which concluded the letter which he wrote to us on May 22, 1910, after the funeral of the great King his father : " With such thoughts I take courage, and hopefully look into the future strong in my faith in God, trusting my people, and cherishing the Laws and Constitution of my beloved Country " ? This morning we put those appealing words the other way round ; we think of the confidence with which his people trust *him*, of the depth of the affection with which his country loves *him*.

We all respect and admire the temper, the courage,

the sense of duty, the impartiality, the human sympathy and understanding with which, in singularly difficult times, he has dealt with the day-to-day responsibilities of his supreme office and faced one crisis after another such as never fell to the powerful personality of King Edward VII to handle. King George has in fact cherished the laws and constitution which belong to us. With a quiet sincerity and the single aim to do on each occasion, great or small, the right thing, he has lived his life and done his incessant work. He has no aim except to do his best for his subjects. Times advance and ways and manners which suit one generation do not match the needs of the next. The rules and the attitude of Queen Victoria to whom the British Empire owes an incalculable debt, would not suit the days in which we live. Adaptations have been necessary, great adaptations since the opening years of this century in which all Englishmen came to confess to one another that in King Edward thay had a Prince after their own hearts and a personal friend. King George has successfully risen to the occasion. Who does not respect him ? Who does not love him as he steps among us again restored from the jaws of death ? Who does not praise God for his recovery ?

We watched and prayed by the side of Her Majesty through those dark weeks of gloom. Our heart goes out to her in this time of gladness ; we wept with the royal family when they wept ; now before God we rejoice with them in their joy.

There is yet one more manner in which King George and his Queen touch the family sense of England. We have been speaking of the family feeling which flows in the blood of all those whom the British Empire embraces. But when our thoughts are turned upon the King we quickly recognize the special appeal that he has made to the affection of his subjects through his own home and home-loving character. The King, his gracious Queen, their sons and their daughters, particularly since the days of the War, have been enthroned in the hearts of the people, because the people, with those family instincts of which we have been speaking, rejoice to look up and find that home life, which is so dear to them, set on high and honoured by their Sovereign and his domestic circle. The King is personally an exponent of the English home in all its strength and beauty. They say that in his home, though of course never off duty, never able to take a complete holiday, he is seen at his happiest and at his best. He is not a man who thirsts for incessant excitement. He enjoys his sport, his reading—when they were younger he read to his children—he cares for his houses and gardens, just as other Englishmen do by habit. He reads his Bible every day. He enters into the company and conversation of his friends. He puts all at their ease with ready talk, grave or gay. We know him in Norfolk as the first of our county squires—perhaps some of us with a depth of individual gratitude and affection. Well may we thank God, with others, perhaps beyond others, for giving us such a King, and to-day for giving him back to us again. *Praise thou the Lord, O my soul.*

PART II

THE ENGLISH CHURCH : YOUTH AND EDUCATION

VIII

THE CHURCH AND YOUTH: ENGLISH HOME LIFE [1]

" Sanctify them in the truth. For their sakes I sanctify myself, that they also might be sanctified. I have no greater joy than to hear that my children walk in the truth."—St. John xvii. 17, 19 ; 3 John 4.

MANY are now making an independent search for truth, and as many are professing to do so. Authority is discredited. This attitude begins in the nursery, it goes on to the lecture-room, it is apparent in common life, it has invaded the Church. Authority is discredited. People will not take things for granted ; in their thoughts and their rules of conduct they do not value the direction of others. They think, or they suppose that they think, they act, or they suppose that they act, on their own initiative.

What can be grander than the search for truth for truth's sake ! What a fine record the last half century has had in this respect. The scientific spirit has been abroad, and to it Nature has yielded up her secrets, and History has disclosed her facts. In the sphere of natural science some estimate these conquests by the conveniences and the adornments of life to which they have led ; for on every side our generation has been enriched with facilities unknown a hundred years ago. Things which then scarcely belonged to the few have now become the property of the many ; and all kinds of things completely unknown before come within the happy range of us all. But I am not dwelling on these great material results which have often come about as a by-product of the search for pure knowledge. I

[1] A sermon preached in the Cathedral Church of Norwich June 3rd, 1929, to welcome the representatives of the Mothers' Union on the occasion of their visit to Norwich.

rather think of the glory attaching to this humble search itself on the part of those who have loved the truth for its own sake.

In the sphere of history, sacred and profane, we might recall similar progress; to give in this place an appropriate example, we may consider the way in which the Bible has become to many a living record. If it had not been for these lovers of the truth it might too largely have admitted of a conventional interpretation, or have been accepted as a mosaic of unrelated fragments, or a storehouse of isolated texts.

It is not, as I have said, all who profess to look for truth who are sincerely devoted to it in this lofty way. Sometimes those who imagine that they are thinking out things for themselves are all the time at the mercy of the group-thinking which dominates the circle in which they move. This applies both to their theories and to their practice. Or again they may seem to themselves to be breaking away from the conventions and trammels of authority, when they are doing no more than repeating the unproved and perhaps conventional assertions of those who have far less claim to allegiance than the old-fashioned authority which, in their over-intelligence, they despise and laugh out of court without any real consideration of what it puts before them. Scraps of information or assertions, made quite irresponsibly and accepted in the same way, will appear to them a sufficient equipment for erecting a new measure of values in their conduct and in their ideas.

Now, let me remark that it would, on the one hand encourage, and on the other hand chasten, and on both hands sanctify our pursuit of truth if one and all we apprehended that all that is true belongs to Him Who is the Truth, and that every real loyalty to truth is loyalty, avowed or unavowed, to Christ. " For this cause came I into the world that I should bear witness

unto the truth. Every one that is of the truth heareth
My voice."

These last words " Every one that is of the truth "
make it clear to us that the truth of which Christ speaks
is something larger than truth of thought and expression
and intellect. Truth, in its fullness, embraces the
spirit and the character ; the body as well as the mind.
The body for instance, corresponds to truth when in
its form and movements it touches the highest to
which it has been called, the loftiest standards set
before it. There is a sisterhood existing between
truth and beauty ; there is a reality of truth ; there is a
reality of beauty. Reality rests in God. Truth and
beauty are different aspects of the way in which God
comes to us. There is a third sister to truth and
beauty, namely, righteousness. We would make a
mistake if we supposed that we could rightly dissociate
righteousness from beauty and truth. Some people
have done this, the people who imagine that ugliness
and unattractiveness or irrationality are bound up
with or even actually commend Christian conduct.
This is wrong ; for on the one side it is for us all, as
St. Peter says, to be able to give a reason of the hope
that is in us, and on the other side we have to remember
the beauty of the life of Him Who is our example ;
our Christian profession should add an attractiveness
to our way of life. There should be nothing repellent
in those who are the faithful followers of Christ.

It was something much greater than accuracy of
observation and precision of statement which St. John
had in his mind when he wrote, " I have no greater joy
than to hear that my children walk in the truth."
There have always been many false standards of conduct in the world ; there have always been, and there
are, false notions of grace and charm and attractiveness ; and thirdly, men and women have constantly
bent their ideas of wisdom and knowledge to correspond
with their own poor ideals, bent them down to the earth

instead of lifting up their thoughts to the glorious, the awful holiness and purity and truth of God. Truth, Righteousness, Beauty have been misconceived.

It is so to-day ; those who seek and speak and act and adorn the truth in love are among the rare ones of the earth. I well know that as you who are mothers look at your children, while they are growing up, or when you forecast what the future has in store for them, you can indeed express your deepest joy, your highest hope, when you can say that your children, your boys and girls, your sons and daughters, as they are reaching to their full-grown life or are already stepping along its path, are keeping clear of the false ways and conceptions and are walking in the truth. You at any rate, can enter into the heart of St. John as, with his mind full of his Master, the Way, the Truth, and the Life, he used these wonderful, these perennial words, " I have no greater joy than that my children walk in the truth." *You* know what he meant, and an old schoolmaster knows too, as he lovingly looks back upon the hundreds and hundreds of boys whom he prepared for Confirmation. Between them and him were forged the tenderest links of association and affection as he and they spoke together of the one Great Master, his and theirs, and St. John's and yours and your children's. As he thinks of them and the way in which their careers are developing now that they have long passed from his hands, he likes to recall those words of allegiance to Christ, the Way, the Truth, and the Life— those words which describe a part of that beautiful conversation in the last chapter of the Gospel of the same St. John :

> " Lord, and what shall this man do ? "
>   Ask'st thou, Christian, for thy friend ?
> If his love for Christ be true,
>   Christ hath told thee of his end :
> This is he whom God approves,
> This is he whom Jesus loves—

and certainly he does not exclude from their application the four hundred and more of his boys who gave their lives in the War.

Let me turn back more closely to our first text. Christ is asking that His disciples should be sanctified in the truth ; that their whole being—body, soul, mind and spirit—may be hallowed in the truth ; their powers and abilities used of God and consecrated ; that the truth, in that widest sense of which we have spoken, may be the very sphere in which they move and have their being. They are not to bow to it here and there, but it is to be like the air they breathe. It is not to be an acquisition nor an accomplishment, nor a characteristic, but the very essence and environment of their whole personality. We are apt to take separately the gifts and faculties of mind and body and spirit, of thought and character. But there is a wholeness in Christ's dealing : He takes us as whole personalities and desires to see our whole selves flooded with the truth of God. In this wondrous passage what does He say that He is Himself doing to promote this great end ? He sanctifies Himself that His disciples also may be sanctified. He offered to God a completely consecrated life, untainted by sin, perfect through sufferings, completely obedient to the Father's will. And Christ is the Head of humanity, the crown of the human race ; and therefore those who are *in Christ* are, through Him, made to share all that He won as the Representative Man. He has redeemed fallen humanity ; He has consummated all the noble capacities of human nature, and He imparts to all His members the virtue of His own achievements. The Holy Spirit takes what belongs to Christ and distributes His gifts among us. Christ did not sanctify Himself in isolated sincerity and holiness. He shares of His best with us and sanctifies us in Himself that we too may be made " holy, harmless, undefiled," that we too, as He did, may walk in the truth. Thanks to His victory, we too may be made more than conquerors through Him that loved us. We may each secure from Him all that we need for our own sanctification, and ask for just that touch of the eternal upon all that we are, and do, and think, that will sanctify it all. We may ask Him, through the Holy Spirit, to infuse into our thoughts, our hopes, our work, our associations together, our whole attitude to ourselves and to others, into our times of heavy responsibilities, into our days of gladness and of gloom, just that little bit of likeness to Him which will set all aglow with the beauty of consecration.

" For their sakes I sanctify Myself." If just now I appealed to you who are mothers to enter into the mind of St. John when he wrote his third Epistle, so I appeal to you, O mothers, again ; and I ask you whether you cannot from afar, as you look round upon your children that are and that are to be, enter into the mind of Christ Himself. For you know that He can enter into yours. He lovingly understood those profound expectations which stirred your deepest soul from the beginning of your grown womanhood. No one else could guess what was moving in your heart of hearts. But to Him all girls and women, no less men and boys, can confide everything without the smallest reserve—only, there was, there is, no reason to speak to Him; for, so great is His tenderness and His fellow-feeling, that He already knew, He already knows all your secrets. Enter into the mind of Christ, for you too are called to sanctify yourselves for the sake of those who are dearest to you ; and, like Christ's sanctification, your sanctification will, in some sense, influence and embrace these others.

Do not think me trivial if I follow in the steps of St. Paul, who more than once, in the opening chapters of an Epistle, has discussed the heavenly places and then at the end has spoken of the simplest domestic duties. I venture to remind you that if you intend

your children to follow Christ you will lead the way
by your own consecration to Him. Do you wish
them to be truthful ?   Then be very careful you do
not tell what is called the harmless lie.   Are they to
be contented with their surroundings, seeing the best
and not the worst in other people ?   Then you will be
neither petulant nor eager to repeat the unkind gossip.
Are they to be industrious at school, to devote themselves to the many fine opportunities which await the
young to-day ?   Then let them see no laziness or
unresponsiveness in yourselves.   Are they to make
much of the splendid and beautiful things in the world
of nature, of books, of art and of men ?   Then let
them see nothing petty in your outlook and your talk.
If you wish to keep up their interest in what is good
and cultured, do not only speak of their distinctions
in games when they come home from school.   And
on the other hand, when they tell you of their triumphs
at school in games and in work and other occupations,
do not brush it aside by that want of interest which
will immediately freeze their confidence.   Your unselfishness to them, your loyalty to Christ, will ennoble
and consecrate your mutual love and companionship.

" For their sakes I sanctify Myself " : will you bear
with me if in conclusion I read to you a passage of
singular insight and charm ?

" How do men become for the most part ' pure, generous,
and humane ' ? By personal, not by logical, influences.
They have been reared by parents who had these qualities,
they have lived in a society which had a high tone, they
have been accustomed to see just acts done, to hear gentle
words spoken, and the justness and the gentleness have
passed into their hearts and slowly moulded their habits,
and made their moral discernment clear ; they remember
commands and prohibitions which it is a pleasure to obey
for the sake of those who gave them ; often they think
of those who may be dead and say, ' How would this
action appear to him ? Would he approve that word, or
disapprove it ? '   To such, no baseness appears a small

baseness because its consequences may be small.   Often in solitude they blush when some impure fancy sails across the clear heaven of their minds, because they are never alone, because the absent Examples, the Authorities they still revere, rule, not their actions only, but their inmost hearts ; because their conscience is indeed awake and alive, representing all the nobleness with which they stand in sympathy, and reporting their most hidden indecorum before a public opinion of the absent and the dead."

Thank God you are not among the absent or the dead.   You are living with your children in your delightful homes, you are creating all around them this beautiful appeal, you are drawing them with the bands of love towards this loftiness and purity of mind.   Sanctifying yourselves for their sakes, you are rearing good men and women to serve our nation and our empire in their generation, in the days to come. You are making to God the best offering which your womanhood, in all the joys and pains, the fears and yearnings, the unreserved selflessness of the mother, can bring to God.   You are storing up for yourselves as a great and eternal reward the consciousness that you have taught your children to walk in the truth.

IX

SCHOOL AND HOME [1]

" We are able. Δυνάμεθα."—St. Matt. xx. 22

IN years gone by, when I was a head master, I found it an exacting task in the summer holidays to make out schemes of work for the ensuing year. To place masters, boys, and subjects correctly, involved some perplexing calculations and dispositions which, with many erasures, developed under my hand. At the time my own study might appear to contain just a pile of papers possessing no human interest. But it was those schedules in their final form which directed every boy and every man to the right spot at every hour of the week for the study of a variety of interests ; and once the true work was set going, of course it was full of life and vivacity.

I say this at the beginning of my sermon, in which it is a delight to me to welcome you all to our Cathedral this morning, lest it should appear that I was unfamiliar with the necessity of educational machinery, and was going on to speak in an unpractical way of the real subject of my sermon.

I have another preliminary remark to make, and it is this, that in discussing education we must be extremely careful not to forget the part which home life ought to sustain in it. The very fact that our public administration is in many departments of life so efficient, leads to the weakening of personal responsibility. While there are some who resent this in various fields, who regard the State as intruding into the privacy of family life, and join the chorus of

---

[1] A sermon preached in the Cathedral Church of Norwich February 22nd, 1925, on the occasion of the jubilee of the Norwich High School for Girls.

persons who exclaim that the country as a whole, and the smaller groups of its citizens, would do better without so much central direction : others, starting from the same consideration, divest themselves of any personal initiative or purpose, and surrender their very own obligations into the hands of public administrators who, of course, cannot discharge them. Certainly in education, home life and school life ought unquestionably to be dovetailed together. Schoolmasters can undertake parts of education which are out of the reach of parents ; but they certainly cannot undertake those parts which are specially the privilege of fathers and mothers. When the influence which should be derived from both these two educational sources acting together fails, then so far the education fails also. I can well remember the illumination it would be to me upon the character-forming—and this is the education—of an individual boy, to meet his father and his mother, and to see whether the home life pulled against all that was noblest in his school life, or whether what we attempted to do at school was backed up at home. But at the moment I am more particularly thinking of the way in which the very elaboration, precision, punctuality, and efficiency of school arrangements do tend to lead thoughtless fathers and mothers to neglect their own duty in rearing and preparing their own children for the good use of the working hours of their grown-up careers, and—what to-day is equally important—for the good use of the leisure hours of their life. Parents who simply content themselves with telling a child not to do this or that in some moment of exasperation are not really evoking what is best in the child, who will really respond to the love and sympathy of a father and mother if they will not just find fault, but quietly and gently guide the growing lives of their boys and girls, and enter into their interests and their new friendships. I am not saying now what is perfectly true, that here is found the secret of a happy home. I am rather urging that it makes a rift in the education of a boy or girl if school and home are not united together in training him or her as the child of God, and as a future citizen of our great Empire. Nor do I think that parents have the least conception of the way in which they can help the schoolmaster and the schoolmistress by taking a little interest on Sunday or weekday in the school lessons, asking in a word or two what the children have been learning, and joyfully sympathizing with any little advance that they may make. By such ways they will not only keep their children nearer to themselves in confidence and love, but will be making a very definite contribution to assist the noble work that goes on within the walls of the school, and should also be carried on, quietly and unobtrusively, in the playgrounds outside.

Now, this morning, to put it shortly, my desire is to view the influence of one personality on another. . . .

Such individual touch does not for a moment deny the nobility of fellowship. The individuals who constitute a noble community make up one great whole ; at the best, both objectively and subjectively great, great not only because of its size, but great in its own sense of unity.

It is then, I say, when the impact of teacher upon pupil strikes a light, that the torch of true education begins to glow. This personal intimacy, though readily belonging to actual teachers and learners, does not necessarily or always come from the living master or mistress. The personality of a great writer reaches through his books many whom he has never seen, or many of a different generation. But still spirit touches spirit through intercourse, through literature ; and Nature herself seems to speak with her own voice, and not as an impersonal power, to charm and guide her devotees.

Organization by itself has little value ; we have to

5

think of the real people who are at the other end of
the line which we draw in our offices. It was said of
Archbishop Benson that one of the things that made
him so great and sympathetic a leader was that in all
his work on committees and in framing policies for
the whole Church, and in all the discussions in which
he had to take his part, he always kept clear before
his mind what this or that would mean, when in the
end it came to touch the actual parishes and the
people living in them.

Spirit must touch spirit. I might, of course, have
gone on to say something on this subject in wide
ranges of life at home and abroad. But limiting
myself to the question which is engaging your attention
in your visit to Norwich, I think I may say that in the
field of education the need of this spiritual contact
between person and person is plain to those who have
watched the progress or the lack of progress of pupils.
The surroundings and the opportunities may appear
exactly the same, yet the man who has a gift for
viewing the tasks set before his pupils as they view
them, and *each* of them views them, will be able to
evoke an interest that is quite beyond the reach of a
master who may know the subject better, but his
pupils less. Every successful teacher of the young
must have this power of entering into the minds of
the young. And it comes not from reading books
about them, but from caring for them. And I may
say, by the way, that I am sure that for all of us to-day
a knowledge of the way in which young people are
looking upon the problems of the hour is all-important.
Nothing will better keep us from trying to impose on
others views which may have helped us in our time,
but make no appeal to the world at large to-day and
have ceased to be effective. I should always like to
have at hand some frank young person to comment
upon everything I write or plan or say, for I know
that I should be the gainer and be brought nearer to

the ever-moving current of thought and hope and purpose in the world. But to return. Some of you know the dreariness of the picture when the wrong man is teaching the wrong thing in the wrong way. This reaches its climax when the teacher does not himself care for what he is teaching, and ends in dictating notes—a melancholy plan exactly calculated to deaden any response on the part of the victims of such a system. But the man or woman who loves the subject with a true love, and finds a personal joy in the progress of each of his pupils, is the one who touches the right spot in them. Under the encouraging influence of that kind of partnership where each is by the side of the other the learner learns with growing, happy self-confidence. There you have spirit touching spirit; and there is light. Of course, this constantly means patience ; but only such patience as our Lord showed when the disciples, whose hearts He knew were really at one with Him, made some of their blundering and foolish remarks.

Then let me go on to speak of the happiness of one who teaches in this way. Many who are present here this morning must know the charm of seeing the development, yes, and often the boyish self-confidence and eager anticipations, of many of the young as they face, in passing ignorance but in lasting enthusiasm, the work that will lie before them in the world.

I can never read often enough the story of the two brothers whose mother approached the Lord Christ and asked for her sons the first place in His Kingdom. " Are ye able," said He, " to drink of the cup that I shall drink of, and to be baptized with the baptism that I am baptized with ? " They say unto Him, " We are able." He did not rebuke them, He only told them that before they would have accomplished their service they would have to learn more than they yet could know of all that was involved in what they had asked : " Ye shall drink indeed of My cup, and be baptized with the baptism that I am baptized with; but to sit on my right hand and on my left, is not mine to give, but it shall be given to them for whom it is prepared of my Father." These last words were, as history proved, no rejection of their offer, for after their youthful enthusiasm had been purified, tested, and concentrated, they were indeed to be judged of His Father, worthy to take a first place in His Kingdom.

We think of the different service these young men rendered—the one slain almost immediately in the cause of Christ, the other living long and giving fuller and fuller witness to the Love of God. And then we old schoolmasters of schools of every kind read in the story the dedication of the varied services to their generation which are or were rendered by the dear boys who sat side by side in the same class-rooms, played in the same fields, lived in the same rooms, worshipped together in the same chapel. Some, like St. James, fell by the sword in the War, others go forward like St. John in the noble work of a lifetime of generous thought and effort. But we thank God for the memory of them all as we have watched, first the blade and then the ear, after that the full corn in the ear.

We are able. And to each and all who have been true to Christ there has come or there will come a reward, though not even the old teacher who possesses the truest foresight or the deepest insight can venture to prophesy the way in which God will use and reward His own.

X

AN ENGLISH GIRL'S RELIGION [1]

" I have called you friends."—St. John xv. 15

YOU may be sure that it is a special joy to me to visit you to-day and to find myself back among the delightful companionships of school life. This happiness is increased when the day of my visit marks one of those pre-eminently bright times when all that is dearest to you in the two parts of your life—the home part and the school part—meet in joyous harmony. To-day you can introduce those whom you love at home to those whom you love at school, and you delight to know that in future your companions will be able to picture some of the persons of whom you have so often spoken to them.

Again, it may be that you will be glad that your parents can to-day assure those who teach you here, who have offered you through your school years a noble ideal of life's possibilities, who fill a place in your heart to which no others will ever quite succeed, of that gratitude which you may find it hard to express with your own lips. And if your father and mother do thus interpret your own glad sense of indebtedness they will, I know, also be voicing the feelings that lie deep in their own hearts.

There are some of you, I suppose, who are now looking back upon the well-nigh completed course of their school career. They regard it with many a wistful regret as they picture all that has passed since they first arrived here with trembling diffidence, and this bright day on which for the last time they take

[1] A sermon preached in the Abbey Church of Sherborne July 7th, 1916, at the Commemoration Service of the Sherborne School for Girls.

part in your Commemoration as present members of your school-fellowship.

Yet, though they part from your company in one sense, in heart and mind they will always be members of this community to the end of their days. When they have homes of their own they will not forget the old friends of days gone by, and a letter from a school friend or a visit from her will touch a tender chord in a manner all its own.

In the Peninsular War, when Count Romana was to be communicated with by his friends who had no means of access to him, the ingenious plan was hit upon that the messenger, who could not dare to carry any credentials through the enemy, should learn by heart certain verses in the composition of which Romana—a man of great taste—had taken a part. The plan was successful; in the messenger Romana recognized a friend by the very personal character of that which he and Romana shared together, secret as it was from the rest of the world. So it is with the love of their school which unites boys or girls, even of different generations, as they meet in later life. The common associations of the past link them together; they all have one place about which they love to speak in a language that would mean nothing to anyone who was not one of the faithful company.

Yes, I repeat, for some of you to-day tears are very near to the smiles; the deepest feelings of our hearts are strangely intermingled. You know that this springtide of your life cannot last for ever, but as you pass another milestone on the way you linger with tender affection and have no wish to hasten too quickly to leave the paths of spring behind.

On the other hand, especially in these stirring times, the elders among you wish to be already up and doing. It seems to some of them that the time of preparation should be exchanged for the time of action; that they ought to be taking a more direct part in the work of their country than is open to a mere schoolgirl.

Here they are quite right ; only let them be sure that in thinking thus they are led by pure purpose and that they have counted the cost. We may easily mislead ourselves as to our motives. A girl may say to herself that she wishes to work in a wider field, when the truth is that she is really only eager for her emancipation from the necessary control of school life, with its wise checks and fixed regulations.

" What is a great life ? " it was once asked, and the answer given was, " A vision seen in youth and carried out in later years." A girl who, in schooldays, has seen such a vision, and now seeks on the threshold of her grown-up life to begin to carry it out, is one whose spirit and purpose we all respect. But, I say, do not let anyone here seek freedom unless that freedom is to be spent in service of some kind. Even among girls who are now busy with War work it is possible to find some, at least, who carry it out for the most part as a diversion, who are more flighty than self-sacrificing, and who exploit for their own ends the relaxations of home routine which the War has brought with it.

The War has made the sweet word " Home " doubly precious in view of all the partings, sometimes those longest partings of all, which it has brought with it. But there is a danger lest at this time of varied activities in War work the members of a family should, through their divergent employments, tend to become more and more independent of the ties of united life, lest the mutual love and courtesy and loving-kindness which have been, and always will be, the greatest adornment of home life should be undervalued, or spoiled, or lost.

We cannot afford at this or any time to let our girls fall below the very highest standard which has been anywhere, at any time, put before them. It is to you

and to the right-minded women of our country that
we look to keep bright for us the tender and the
solemn side of war. Men perhaps are too near the
fray, or the preparation for it, to be able to rise higher
or to probe deeper than the actualities of a fierce
conflict. It has been truly said that the methods of
war are, by their very character, such as to throw into
the foreground the material forces and to disparage
the spiritual. But the girls can do much to keep the
atmosphere pure : by their prayer, their sweetness,
their affectionate ways, their loving hearts, their tears
of sorrow and of generous pride, they can lift up our
hearts from the sordid places of the earth to the
heavenly places in Christ Jesus.

Something of all this has been put before you within
these walls. Keep it bright and beautiful when you
have passed from school. I know it is not always
easy for girls to carry with them to their homes and to
their duties and their pleasures *there* the best that they
have made their own at school, without any of the
alloy which necessarily can be easily picked up, by
those who wish to do so, from the weaker side of school
life. Foolish girls, instead of enhancing all those dear
qualities which make us admire them and love them
at home, can, if they so please, unlearn at school some
of that sympathy and tenderness, that affectionate-
ness and demonstrativeness which made them shine
as very sunbeams in their homes. They can become
curt and rough and ready, and even regard it as a
mark of strength and independence to discard the
simplicity and gentleness which added so pretty a
grace to the first years of girlhood at home.

The girls we want to-day are those who have not
lost any of the bloom or the winning look and manner
which made the delight, and the beauty of their home
life, and yet have now added the strength and purpose
and the clear vision which will enable them to help us
without the least shock to our sensibilities.

This I know is not an easy point to reach, but where better shall we seek for those who shall attain it than among girls reared like yourselves in good homes and at a good school ?

These are the girls who, younger or older, evoke all that is best in the boys and the men whom they meet now or will meet in the near years to come. These are the girls whose brothers adore them, and who do far more than they know—yes, and far far more than the brothers themselves know—to keep them simple-hearted, manly, pure, generous, and brave. If you ask an old schoolmaster to say what are the influences most likely to assist a growing boy to be true to his best self, he would put high upon the small list of such holy things a mutual and devoted affection between a brother and a sister which admits of no secrets in holiday time and is maintained by loving letters during the term. Such sisters as I try to speak of are those who justify the advice given by school-masters to their boys, " If you wish to make the most of your time at school, and to protect your memory against haunting regrets, make it your rule never to take part in anything, to do nothing, to say nothing, that you will not be glad to share with your favourite sister when the holidays come. Have no guilty secret in your heart which you could not bear to reach and stain her white and loving heart."

My friends of to-day, we often hear it now said that the War is, at its end, to bring in a new England— new in countless ways. Now, the working out of all this great future will rest with you and your con-temporaries. We who are older will not live to see what you and the men whom you will love shall work out in the family life, the social life, the political and religious life, of our dear England. It is plain that women, who at the time of this crisis have proved their capacity and their devotion, will count for more and more in the years to come. Thank God for that, if they can help the men, without losing anything of what is their own particular charm, if they can help forward the good of the world at large without in any way spoiling the beauty of their home life. To you, my friends, is this trust committed. Some who are older, and who have lived more than half their life, look with envy upon those who have the making of the future in their hands and the gathering of the noblest fruits of the War. I am not one of them. I rather rejoice to think this responsibility is yours and not mine. We each have our allotted span of work, and we must not try to cross the borders. Only, as I see you start forth to do what I shall not be asked to do, and could not do as you can, I ask to give you my blessing before you set out.

Of one thing I am sure, that it is just in proportion as you consecrate the hopes of these earlier years and the powers that you feel springing up within you to the Lord Jesus Christ Himself, that your work will be successful, your lives happy, your influence uplifting and lovely, and your homes—those homes of your own, which one by one you and another will build up together in united love—your homes will become very shrines where God may dwell, blessing you and yours and making you a blessing.

And if I am correct let us, outright, claim for Christ to-day all those things which we respect and admire and love in the girlhood and womanhood of our country, and which in many respects have been so splendidly exhibited in this time of stress and strain. Do not let us be content with any service that only indirectly acknowledges the inspiration of Christ, the example of His life, and the supremacy of our Ascended Lord. We know that all this care for the sick and feeble and for every one who needs a helping hand dates, in its present form, from the new light which Christ brought into the world. But I ask that your connexion with Him should not be just through the ties of history and unacknowledged imitation. Rather in His name I beg you to bring all the capacities with which God has endowed you and to lay them with conscious devotion and tender love at the feet of Him Who " came not to be ministered into, but to minister, and to give His life a ransom for many."

Place your hand in His and He will lead you on, the youngest, the oldest alike. He will lead you with sure steps through these glad years of preparation at school, and in the larger world outside : He will lead you to follow Him lovingly, faithfully still, until at last—oh, the joy of such a reward—the smile of His approval greets you when you meet, face to face, Him whom you have chosen from childhood onward to be through all your life your own Master and your own Friend, your adorable and adored Companion on the high-road of life.

XI

PUBLIC SCHOOL RELIGION [1]

A GENERALIZATION on the subject of religion in public schools can be little more certain and helpful than a generalization with reference to religion in parishes. In either case the conditions must vary very much. For example, there is a broad line which divides the life of a boy in a boarding-school from the life of a boy in a day-school, who spends his Sundays at home, and, if his is a godly family, has Christian teaching and the example of Christian lives constantly put before him. One of the highest spiritual influences that a boy can enjoy is the companionship of his mother and sisters in a good home, and from these advantages the boy in a public school is cut off for three-quarters of the year. When I was a schoolmaster I noticed that the more serious lapses in conduct took place towards the end of a term, and among other reasons for this I placed the fact that " the spell of home affection " was then weakest.

It will then be understood that in what I write I am thinking of my own happy life in days gone by when I was a schoolmaster, and found that the religious aspect of my work constituted quite the best part of it. I cannot speak with any real insight of other boys and other methods than those I knew, though I must frankly acknowledge that there are other manners of influencing boys of which I have heard as employed in other schools that, I believe, might have been adopted to the advantage of the boys in my own old school. I will be boldly egotistical, otherwise I fear I should not be clear and definite, nor my survey in any sense vivid.

[1] An Article published in the *Manchester City News* June 2nd, 1917.

Before I go further perhaps I should observe that in a great public school there is practically no " religious question " in the usual and lamentable meaning of the word. Some few boys are withdrawn from the chapel services or divinity lessons ; but there is nothing in the nature of suspicion or religious cleavage among either parents or boys. I know, however, that the Bible lesson, like other subjects which are supposed not to pay, has to maintain its position against the demand for only " useful " studies. But in this point, as in others, the head master can be a benevolent autocrat, and can usually hold his own if he means to do so.

I may add that I do not believe that questions of the higher criticism and of up-to-date teaching on the literary side of the Bible produce either difficulty or suspicion, provided that such teaching is offered in a really reverent spirit ; for boys are shrewd critics, and can quickly catch the meaning of the sneer of an irreverent or agnostic master.

I have no doubt that the majority of boys expect some religious teaching in their school life, and some opportunities of joint worship, such as are provided in the school chapel. The actual lessons in the classroom and the prayers and the sermons in the chapel may, at any given time, be a weariness to them, and leave them rather bored than inspired. But I believe that many boys would really miss it if religious teaching were omitted from the programme, and more still if the chapel services were discontinued. It is for the most part some of the older boys getting towards the age of leaving school who begin to suggest that it would be an improvement if the chapel services were voluntary.

Sometimes, if it fell early, we spent Easter at school, and then in Holy Week we did have additional short, voluntary services which were well attended by the boys. They used to go into the chapel for ten minutes in the evening ; and with a few prayers I would read to them appropriate passages from Farrar's *Life of Christ*. I was glad to see that they cared so to spend those sacred days.

I certainly do not believe that it is fair to say that the religious ideal of most boys does not rise above a spirit of sportsmanship and good-fellowship and an adherence to the conventional code of honour prevailing among them. I am sure that I was not alone in my own schooldays in looking forward to the weekly sermon from Dr. Haig Brown, that prince of head masters. Things no doubt have moved on since I was a boy at school, and in preparing us for confirmation he taught us more about the Decalogue [*sic*] and the landing of St. Augustine in England than would be appropriate for the modern boy. But his sermons were for all time, and we felt it. And the last of them, which, as a schoolboy, I heard him preach, I constantly read and re-read to this day, copied out as I possess it, in his own handwriting—what a gracious act from a head master to one of his pupils !

I am inclined to think that, as certainly ought to be the case, it is the preparation for Confirmation, and the Confirmation itself, which are richest in influence upon a boy's religious life. There was something very touching in the stillness of the attention with which the boys would listen when, for example, one attempted to speak of manfully fighting against the world, the flesh, and the devil, especially as the middle member of that triumvirate of temptation came into view. But I have often been struck with the way in which they seemed to care to follow a full, if simple, doctrinal exposition, for instance, of the meaning of the Blessed Sacrament. It was a joy to see every boy who was to be confirmed for a talk of ten minutes or a quarter of an hour by himself ; the boys were so trustful and simple and ready to be helped. And every year when the anniversary of the confirmation came round the boys who had been confirmed could, if they pleased, come and renew the previous talks—and very many did, especially the older ones. No one suffered from the hands of his neighbours from being openly summoned at his own suggestion from the classroom to my house. Twice a year all who had been confirmed used to meet in what, in these days, would have been called a " Corporate Communion." We did not call it that, and perhaps we were right, for the service which unites His people to Christ, and to one another in Him, must everywhere and always, and not only on special occasions, be corporate.

While they were at school there were few who gave up coming regularly, on some little rule of their own, to Holy Communion. Here the schoolmaster has a great advantage over the parish priest ; even when his boys have been confirmed at the later age, when they are old enough to know something of the difficulties of life, the former can have time to train them in communicant habits before they go out into the world.

In the lessons in the classroom personality counts for everything. Masters who make no secret of their dislike of teaching such a subject naturally teach little religion in the Scripture hour. Some of them take refuge in elaborating the unspiritual side of the lesson. The Acts of the Apostles has been called " The Gospel of the Holy Spirit " ; but it is easy to treat it as a handbook, with illustrations, of the Roman Provincial Government. To safeguard, in a small way, the spiritual side of the lessons in other forms my practice was to insert in every examination paper two definitely spiritual questions, so that neither boys nor masters should be tempted to lose the wood for the trees.

With the upper boys, some forty in number, I used to delight in dealing with such subjects as the Creed, the Catechism (explained more deeply than to children), Church history, besides books of the Bible. I know I often went over their heads, and yet I was

constantly amazed at the care and the intelligence of
the work which they showed up in examination ; and
that, though I have never believed in the practice of
supplying notes to be learnt more or less by heart.
This has always seemed to me a very poor method of
instruction, destitute of inspiration or any personal
spell, though occupying the time of the class for
a master who is ignorant or afraid of the subject of
the lesson.   Archbishop Temple—that famous head
master—did not believe in unexamined work, and I
endorse his view.

I must not omit the Bible-reading scheme which
many of the boys used daily. When they had been
with us ten days I used to have a little talk with the
new boys of each term in the chapel, urging them
never to do at school anything that they would not
be proud to talk about to their mothers and sisters
when the holidays came—which then seemed so sadly
far in the future. I would ask each of them to take
one of these Scripture-reading booklets, and a second
one also to send home, if he thought that his mother
would like to be reading every day the same piece as
her boy.

I think it will be seen from what I have written
how strongly my own view is in favour of clerical head
masters where they may be had. The first duty of a
head master is to teach—so Archbishop Benson urged
upon me. And if he is to teach he must be a scholar
in the widest sense, who knows and loves his subjects,
and has some contagious enthusiasm for them. Then
he must be an organizer, and possess gifts of administration and other commanding qualities. But I can
never see why these capacities should on the professional side be any the less, if they are solemnly consecrated and illumined by the grace of Holy Orders.
I am sure if I possessed any influence with my boys in
religious, or indeed in other respects, it was in part
because, in an intuitive way that they could not have

analysed, they recognized that I had been commis-
sioned from on high and ordained to do the work that
I tried to do among them; and they felt, and I knew,
that on both sides this gave us a right to approach
one another in the things that matter most without
any awkward reserve. Hundreds of them have now
fallen in the War, and as I look back upon the gladness of those days, when I was associated with those
who remain and those who have passed over, I find that
it came from the fact that we were not only friends,
but friends in the Lord. I have a fancy that this
feeling was, and is, mutual. From my heart I thank
God for it.

XII

PUNISHMENT, HUMAN AND DIVINE [1]

"A Prince and a Saviour."—Acts v. 31

THE Church's year is drawing to its close; to-day is a day of retrospect. Next Sunday tells us to look forward to the coming of the Lord for judgment. Which of us, as we look back to the past, can be satisfied? And as we look to the future we cannot pass by Christ's coming to judge as having no reference to us. And the anticipation of judgment leads us on further to the thought of punishment, with its present and future meaning for ourselves and others. I ask, then, to-day . . . to speak of punishment, human and divine. It is a difficult subject and it is hard to discover what are and what ought to be the various elements contributed by thought and emotion to a correct conception of it. To some minds and in some places one or other item of the whole is the more prominent, but the thing itself carefully interpreted combines many aspects into one, since, for example, we must note that in more than one relation it looks in two directions: it looks to the society and the individual, to the past and the future, to the law broken and to the law breaker.

Now I suppose that the first idea of punishment that springs to our mind is that he who does wrong must suffer for it. Bishop Butler, on the nature of virtue, remarks: "There is in human creatures an association of the two ideas, natural and moral evil, wickedness and punishment. If this association were merely artificial or accidental, it were nothing; but being most unquestionably natural, it greatly concerns us to attend to it, instead of endeavouring to explain

[1] A sermon preached in the Temple Church November 20th, 1921.

it away." That is a truth—for it is a truth—that animates some of the great Greek tragedies. There is a majesty in law in the widest sense of that term, and violated law demands that one who has insulted it shall be brought to recognize through suffering that its sovereignty must be maintained. Sometimes he who is punished will himself understand this, and, as he looks back upon his fault, may welcome the penalty, feeling that the bearing of it sets him right again with the outraged authority, just as disobedient dogs will be glad to take their beating and to be restored to favour ; and when his frame of mind in this way brings the penitent wrongdoer across from the side of sympathy with the wrong action to the side of sympathy with the law which he has broken, with the punisher who defends the law, he is on the road to forgiveness. We must, however, note that the conception of punishment as vindicating the law which has been broken can readily degenerate into mere vindictiveness. This happens when more prominence is given to the suffering of the offender than to the reason and aim of his punishment.

Another element in punishment is the redress of wrongs inflicted. This is often impossible. A man who takes another's life cannot restore it, but one who takes another's property may be able to do so. But we justly regard it as a proper evidence of repentance that one who regrets the wrong he has done should, so far as he is able, be eager to make reparation.

Thirdly, we regard punishment as warning. We are right when we urge that the spectacle of the consequences of wrongdoing, not only those which result in the heart of the wrongdoer, but those which are inflicted from the outside, will act as a deterrent to himself and to others not to pursue the actions which have led to such disaster. For there are some men—not all—who will be less ready to commit an offence if they have tasted or watched the experience of the punishment which follows, bearing in mind that the same painful experience will follow a repetition of the same bad conduct.

In the fourth place, the reformation of the individual is a part of punishment ; perhaps the part of which we chiefly think in our generation. Punishment, we feel, ought to be of such a character that it will not brutalize but improve the offender. It has even been supposed that capital punishment has this effect among others ; I do not refer to the preparation for death in this form, such as I have more than once come into touch with in confirming a condemned criminal before his execution ; what I rather mean is that it may be that in a flash, at the moment of death, a reformatory power prevails. But that is by the way. In other cases, at any rate, punishment is viewed, perhaps primarily, as intended to lead the guilty from a bad past to a better future. It is to be like the wisely-tempered chastening of benevolent parents whose motive in disciplining their children is not only to repress evil tendencies but also to strengthen their children's character and to develop all that is good in them. To such punishment the recipient of it may or may not respond. If he does respond, it will certainly help him, and where punishment does have this reforming effect the individual will be thankful for the process. This reforming punishment looks rather to the future than to the past, and its danger is that its supporters may determine the treatment of those who are to be reformed so completely by the future hope as almost to ignore the fault or the wrongdoing. Such a system of punishment can be exploited by those who have not the least intention to be reformed and may find that the surroundings of punishment are so tender as to be preferable to their present environment, just as there are said to be habitual criminals who like to spend the summer out and about, and the winter in gaol where there is regular food and warmth to be had in spite of its other

hardships.   There is, I believe, a real danger if in the
enthusiasm for this reforming power of punishment the
first point of which I spoke, namely, the punishment
due to him who violates the majesty of the law, is
wholly forgotten : for, in a fifth sense, punishment must
not be of such a sort as to consider only the erring
individual, and to ignore those whom he has hurt.

I am speaking now of more than redress.   I am
thinking of the importance of punishment protecting
the community from the attacks of wicked men.   I do
not say that this fifth head is independent of the others ;
indeed, all these various points are so closely intermingled that it is difficult to isolate one from the rest.
But now I am thinking of those who, by a misapplica-
tion of Christ's words, that we are to love our enemies,
speak as if any punishment but that inflicted by the
conscience is out of place.   But what our Lord inculcated is the spirit of forgiving our own enemies, not
treating in a feeble way the enemies or assailants of
other people.   Too often, I fear, a man or a group of
people, commit some hideous wrong, and then, owing
to some failure to picture what they have done or the
harm they have inflicted upon the community, a
sentimental protest is raised that such people should be
spared :   the wrongdoers are almost turned into heroes
and their victims are forgotten.   Punishment in a case
of this kind is a duty laid upon society as a whole for
the support of those who have been exposed to such
outrage, and the protection of those who will be exposed
to it, if it is left unchecked.

Now to turn to the important question of the mind
of the punisher and the punished.   First, we observe
the difference made by the capacity of the punished
to understand and interpret their treatment.   I have
already said that considerate reformatory treatment
will be abused and cynically made to serve their own
ends by some degraded natures.   Savages who work
against the law of nations, as the Romans called it,

have to be taught by painful suffering to behave better, for they are unable to appreciate reformatory methods. Only punishment that is in the form of fear will bring them into the right path. This is the reason of punitive expeditions where the innocent suffer with the guilty. No one desires the innocent to suffer with the guilty ; but if, in an imperfect world, such punitive expeditions are the only known way to prevent graver calamities, if this is the only form of judgment that can be understood, provisionally and for the time being, this is the form that must be used. We do not in so acting outrage any moral sense in the savages' heart ; and if we ourselves have any qualms in our hearts, these qualms become only regrets when we dwell upon the considerations which I have just urged. Some day we trust the savage will be lifted to a loftier and less animal stage ; but, at the moment, it is no use to make any appeal or to employ any treatment that will necessarily be misunderstood. If some uncivilized tribe, by their very nature regard kindness as weakness and nothing else, kindness in their case ceases to be what we intend by kindness. But we must, as soon as ever possible, catch the first gleam of a dawning consciousness of higher things, and act so as quickly to develop it. It would be a very difficult question to determine at what point, if ever, a civilized people had so far returned to the opinions and ways of the savage that it can only be appealed to by the one method which the savage understands.

This last point leads us on to speak of the less hypothetical subject of reprisals, which, however, stand on rather a different footing from the punitive expedition. If they are to be justified, a strong element in their justification must be found in the consideration that those innocent who suffer are not in many cases so completely innocent after all ; for often these innocent persons, though they may take no active part in the wrongdoing which evokes the punishment, yet are contributors to the public opinion which stands behind and presses forward the wrong action. I think it was Archbishop Benson who said that the sins of society show themselves in individuals, and, therefore, the society is largely responsible for these individual sins. In some such spirit, before now, when I was a school-master, have I punished a large number of boys for the offence of the undetected culprit hidden among them, telling them, and telling them truly, that if the whole group had condemned the action it never would have been perpetrated, and I have seen the success of such treatment in lifting the tone of the community : there is no reason why, when it is properly explained, it should cause any bitterness or sullen sense of injustice.

Next we look at the frame of mind of the authority which inflicts punishment. No one is fit to punish who himself at the time feels any sense of personal and private anger. His attitude must be wholly detached ; he must view the whole case fairly and, if necessary, balance evenly the rights of individuals and of society, the requirements of the past and of the future, the aspects—perhaps conflicting aspects—of retribution and redress and of reformation. He must be utterly free from vindictiveness ; he must find no sense of satisfaction in the infliction of pain. Such a temper is very far indeed removed from the usual style of the popular clamour for punishment ; in that there is often nothing judicial and only a violent animosity which lays more stress upon the means than the end, which in cases where it demands a victim may even gloat over the prospect of retaliatory cruelty, and forget the proper dignity of punishment.

And now, having seen the difficulties and perplexities involved in the use of the instrument of punishment in the hands of men, we pass to speak briefly of punish-ment from the Divine side, so far as we can apprehend it.

First, we must remember that God is omniscient and

combines perfect wisdom and love, that He sees the end from the beginning. Therefore, He Who knows all can deal with forgiveness and punishment as we, who know so little, could not dare to do. Our plans of punishment, in consequence, must necessarily be conceived differently from His.

Secondly, however, this does not mean that great principles of truth and justice which we have clearly seen with our eyes as rightly governing our own conduct can be supposed to be set aside by God in punishment. We cannot for a moment imagine that we could regard as appropriate to God anything which would be morally wrong in ourselves.

Thirdly, I would say that both these considerations must affect our view of Christ's Atonement. It relates to a transaction which has its efficacy in the eternal world as well as its place in human history of which the Crucifixion with the Resurrection is the central point. This eternal element in it makes it impossible for us to think that we can with our finite minds grasp the whole ; whatever terms we use are those of illustration or symbol, not those of precise or logical definition. We must not, however, as I remarked a moment ago, attribute any plan to God which would outrage our human ideas of justice. We cannot, therefore, speak of the Son of God as interposing as an innocent sufferer between the wrath of God and its victims while this blind wrath cares not whom it strikes. Those who say that the Christian doctrine of the Cross involves such a statement have taken little pains to hear what the Church to-day is saying on the subject. To-day we have let pass that theory which, so far as it has prevailed, has been only a very limited illustration of one partial aspect of the truth. Calvary is not for us the scene of vengeance : we see there the love of Christ and equally the love of the Father Who spared not His own Son, but delivered Him up for us all. We rather speak of Christ dying as the Representative of

the whole human race, which finds its corporate
personality in Him, dying on behalf of us His brethren,
and through that death reconciling us to God. So in
Him we find the forgiveness of sins ; hence comes the
great multitude, which no man can number, of those
who have " washed their robes and made them white in
the blood of the Lamb." From another side of the
same truth, if it is another, we are taught to cry,
" Behold the Lamb of God, which taketh away the sin
of the world." Sin was the barrier between man and
God, and Christ, by bearing it Himself, as the Head of
humanity, has borne it away and removed it.

In the fourth place, this last statement of the truth
leads us to say one word upon the difference between
sin and punishment. His Name was " called Jesus
because He should save His people from their sins."
When we come into the presence of God, our hearts
tell us that, when we are thinking of punishment as
pain inflicted to vindicate God's law, it is the sin itself
which is sin's real punishment, for it keeps us from God,
and that is the bitterest of penalties. And, on the
other hand, we can see that any discipline, external or
internal, however painful, coming from a Father's love,
may be the best hope of the sinner to bring him back
to God. In this matter we often speak confusedly
about sin and punishment. We ask for the removal of
the discipline instead of the removal of the sin itself in
which is the true sting ; and that removal of sin can
only be achieved by this chastening. We must not
confound two things, both of which we have seen to be
elements of punishment, namely, the reformatory
chastening and the retributory penalty, which latter,
as I say, is in the sin itself. The chastening part of
punishment accepted as chastening, in removing the
sin will remove its own burning self-punishment.
" This is life eternal," said the Lord, " that they might
know thee, the only true God and Jesus Christ whom
thou hast sent." The opposite of life eternal is the

outer darkness which belongs to those who refuse to know and follow God ; and so long as they refuse to know God the outer darkness is self-chosen. It is at once their sin and its necessary penalty. If they were wise they would welcome any road, however hard, that will bring them back to light and life, to life eternal in the knowledge of God.

And what, my brethren, is the main upshot of these things to us on this last Sunday of the Christian year ? Just this : that we have a Saviour if we will turn to Him, in Whom first we can find pardon and peace, a Saviour too to save us from sin, from sinning, and thus, and only thus, from the consequences of sin, retributory or reformatory ; a Saviour to save us from all that is unworthy of the children of God ; a Prince and a Saviour, to transfer our allegiance from the side of sin to the side of the service of God and man. The first of English hymns tells us of the double release, the double remission of sins, effected by this our Prince and Saviour ; one verse of it is more eloquent than all my sermon :

> Rock of ages cleft for me,
> Let me hide myself in Thee ;
> Let the water and the blood,
> From Thy riven side which flowed,
> Be of sin the double cure,
> Cleanse me from its guilt and power.

PART III
DOCTRINE IN THE ENGLISH CHURCH

XIII

PROOF AND FAITH [1]

" Increase our faith."—Luke xvii. 5

THERE are, I think, many men who, being true
adherents of our Lord Jesus Christ, at times
find themselves passing through a phase of religious
experience which asks for a greater confirmation of
their faith.   I am not speaking of those who have never
had any real faith in the revelation of God in Christ,
nor of those who, as they have grown older, through
the mental difficulties that they have met, have so far
deserted their original beliefs that they have come
honestly to doubt the Christian position.   I do not
address my words to any such, and indeed I am sure
that, in many respects, such as these would consider
that I was in this sermon over and over again begging
the question.   I am thinking of those who have never
lost the love and adoration of Christ from their heart,
and classing themselves, in spite of many failures, as
true servants of our Lord Jesus Christ, yet have now
begun to wonder why a fuller light is not allowed to
them, and to wish that they had more in the shape of
outward arguments to sustain their inward beliefs.
Sometimes I have no doubt that the people whom I
have thus attempted to characterize do find themselves
exposed to a further distress, and come to inquire
whether, after all, they are true believers, and whether
the misgivings they have felt, and the lack of outward
certainty from which they are suffering, do not, in
spite of all their wishes to the contrary and in spite of
their sense of adherence to Christ, indicate that they
ought to be ranked among the doubters and unbelievers.

[1] A University sermon preached in Great St. Mary's Church,
Cambridge, May 14th, 1911.

Some men, I fancy, have met with this trial at the end of a long life of true service to Christ, and at any rate I can think of one published biography across which such a dark shadow is seen to have fallen. To some men this phase of distress is only too likely to come as they are beginning to question the earlier beliefs of boyhood and manhood, when in a new way, for the first time, they come to close quarters with those who are unquestionably doubters.

It may be that some of my hearers are conscious in themselves of the symptoms which I have indicated, or can in some one in whom they are interested recognize the picture which I have attempted to draw.

I think such a frame of mind has to be considered very tenderly, with words of encouragement and not of reproof. It is true that such people in regard to their convictions might fall under St. Paul's condemnation of having begun in the spirit, and yet now desiring to be made perfect by the flesh; and yet I think he would have extended to them that large-hearted sympathy which went out from him to those who, unlike the Galatians, had not changed their faith, but were suffering from an excess of conscientiousness or scrupulosity, and tormenting themselves because they had failed to see the proportion of religious things, and to assign their respective importance to the various *strata*, if I may so call them, on which the Christian life rests its foundations.

In the first place, when we deplore that we possess no greater or more convincing outward evidence to support our faith we must observe that we are already forgetting that universal rule of the Christian life to which in general we give an unqualified adhesion that " we walk by faith, not by sight." We forget that in making such a claim for more and brighter signs to guide us we are attempting to justify the heavenly by the earthly, and ignoring the fact that that which is born of the flesh is flesh; and that which is born of the

Spirit is spirit. If we want to make stronger our grasp on heavenly things by mere earthly arguments, the result of the process would be of the earth, earthy, and so far from better substantiating the heavenly truths, we should only have dragged them down from the heights and brought them within the compass and the measurements of earth, and changed and degraded their heavenly character, and our own highest aspiration towards them.

Again, to return to that which I just said about the *strata* of our convictions, a difficulty may present itself to our mind and be one to which we are unable to give a satisfactory reply, and yet all the time it may be really irrelevant to our deeper faith : it may relate to the region of sight and its solution may be beyond our view. Many of the puzzles that beset a devout mind are of this character : puzzles of which the solution, if it were given, would not really enlarge the power of faith.

For example, a young man has always accepted our Lord's Incarnation, and believes that in it he has seen God come into the life of man. In this faith he has lived, and it has justified itself by the light and the strength which it has brought with it. He has again and again verified this truth by the results which he has seen it to effect in his own life and in the life of the world around. It has commended itself in the innermost shrine of his heart, where he has in all humility with St. Paul been able to say, " I live ; yet not I, but Christ liveth in me : and the life which I now live in the flesh I live by the faith of the Son of God, who loved me, and gave Himself for me." So far he has not puzzled himself with the manner of the Incarnation. Now he finds himself among new people ; he sees that they do not possess his simple faith, and are in doubt as to the reality of the Incarnation. He recognizes that they are disinclined to accept its truth before they have definitely satisfied their minds as to its possibility ;

this they have not done.   Perhaps they ask him if he, a true believer, can explain the Incarnation.   He cannot : he feels at a loss ; he wonders if he has been credulous and shortsighted ; he thinks that he ought to be able to give a reason of the hope that is in him. He is distressed ; the truth that he has been holding is no less true to him, and yet it seems as if a cloud were passing between its light and him.

He fails to see that he is confusing things that move in different regions.   It is quite possible to discuss the Incarnation from the metaphysical side, and to consider all that may be said upon such a topic ; but it is certainly untrue to suppose that only those who have cleared the intellectual ground can adore the Incarnate Christ.   Probably the furthest that can be reached from the philosophical side is that the Incarnation is fully credible and admits of justification or illustration and removes as many difficulties as it introduces ; but even if we could go much further towards certitude by the use of our unaided minds, we should still be on a different *stratum* from this young man's early belief. How far away from the joy of friendship which leads us to turn to our friend in our need are theories about the possibility of friendship ! A child's love of its mother moves in a different plane from the evidence that can prove that she and not another is its mother. In many departments of life we can easily puzzle ourselves over our cogitations, while all the time our action is quite straightforward and clear.

The answer of faith to the gospel story is really independent of speculative difficulties, which are necessarily insuperable and insoluble.   It is, indeed, a mistake to think that faith is wavering when it is merely the voice of our intellects which is simply silent in face of a great truth which transcends but does not contradict their highest flights.

If we read the gospel story we shall find that it is our needs which give us the eyes with which to see

Christ. The eyes of the pure in heart are those which see God ; love sees farther and deeper than intellectual skill. Otherwise it would be only the learned, the clever, who could come with confident hope to Christ ; and yet when Christ was upon our earth these were the very ones who found it most difficult to recognize Him. The faith of the little child is that which He asked for, that He might reveal Himself to it. "He that hath my commandments, and keepeth them, he it is that loveth me : and he that loveth me shall be loved of my Father, and I will love him, and will manifest myself to him."

The satisfaction of a need, not the demonstration of an argument, produced the trustful, loving, life-changing confession. We think of the fishermen mending their nets who first heard Christ's call, we think of the woman who was a sinner, of the widow of Nain, of Zacchæus, of Matthew the publican, of the nobleman, of the woman with the issue of blood, of the centurion, of the Syrophœnician woman, and we recognize that it was their needs which opened their eyes to accept in faith and love the Saviour Whom they required. And then we seem to find that we are beginning at the wrong end if we try to lead ourselves up to Christ by philosophical arguments and reasoned demonstrations, and that here in His presence we have reached a place where proof follows sight and does not precede it. Such humble folk as we have enumerated turned their eyes away from any intellectual effort which they might have made—and very likely it would have been a very feeble one—and fixed their gaze on Him who justified His claim by what He did to *them*, by what He became to them. In many cases it is probable that such people as these did not trouble themselves much about proofs when they had seen the Desire of their eyes.

And even when we come to consider the more thoughtful writings of the New Testament, our own

7

habitual way of looking at the matter may lead us to be surprised that the Apostles, instead of proving their point, assume it, and then illustrate it ; and rather leave us with the impression that they felt, " It must be so," than lead us forward step by step in argument to say ," Therefore it is so."   Many have noticed before now how the Christology of the New Testament is developed in such an incidental way, and that the contributions to the unfolding of the apostolic doctrine of the Person of our Lord, in most cases, derives itself from a discussion of simple, loving adherence and obedience to Him.   When *we* lay all the stress upon the proof which we can discover for our minds in that which the New Testament writers have declared of Christ, we are really reading their writings backwards and beginning at the other end to that from which they started.

Proof, I repeat, follows sight, and the Lord's invitation to us, as to John's disciples when He saw them following, is not " See and come," but " Come and ye shall see."   If, then, we are startled at one time or other of our life to find that we have been laying a greater stress upon the coming than on the reasoned processes of the seeing, we need not be distressed, we have not acted amiss ; we have not been credulous, we have not been untrue to the powers of intellect and investigation which God has given us ; we have been keeping the order of action which belongs to little children ;   we   have   been   keeping   Christ's   order, Christ's rule.   If, again, when we have emerged from the simple beliefs of childhood, accepted without question from those whom we have loved, we find ourselves face to face with those who have gone further than we have in proving and testing, this new atmosphere in which we find ourselves is not to confute us, as if so far we had been all wrong, as if so far we had been travelling on the wrong track.   It should only stir us to hold all the closer as our very own the treasure which we already possess, and make us see more plainly its true value. For such a new influence will of course exercise a really wholesome discipline upon us if it further prevents our being content with mere tradition, mere routine, with other people's thoughts, and makes even more deeply the Christ of our home to become the Christ of our hearts, Whom we are more and more to love and adore with a personal and independent devotion.

If Christ is already our own—and I am not speaking to those whose attitude to Him so far has been one of merely conventional religion—we have no reason to be distressed because of the simplicity of our faith, or because we find others questioning that which is to us the very first assumption of all our life. We need not trouble our heads because we have not accustomed ourselves to try to see very far into the dimness ; our circle of reasoned apprehension may not be a very wide one, but we have no reason to doubt the light that shines immediately under the Cross of Christ because we have not strained our eyes to pierce the darker horizon into which we ourselves need never step.

It is so with young children, that they will haunt with familiar footsteps places which they know well and where they are happy, and will be almost terrified if they step beyond this restricted little area where they are at home ; and the place in which they are happy and comfortable is the place in which they remain. Thus, too, with ourselves, we need not discredit that place of faith where we have been and are, because we are timid to travel out into the unknown. At any rate, we need not make the foolish mistake of saying to ourselves that we will not any longer be happy in the one safe place which we know, because we feel that all round us there is a strange, unknown, difficult country from which, if we could reach it, the view of this our spot of safety might be different from that vision of it which we who are upon it have learnt to love and trust.

But, in conclusion, if we are regretting that God has not come closer into our life and that the things that belong to Him seem far away from us, and if we are regretting that the connexion between this world and the other world, as we speak, is not more demonstrably close, are we not all the time forgetting the unquestioned ways in which a contact is already maintained between the things which are seen and the things which are not seen? It is a common weakness for people to ask for more than they possess, and, in their desire for that which they have not got, to underestimate the greatness or the importance of that which is already their own. If they had started with half of that which they have, and then some one gave them the other half, they would be amply pleased, but starting with the whole they consider it is insufficient. And this is the case in regard to the things of God : if the signs that He has truly given us came to us as something new we should be surprised at their fullness ; but having had them in front of our eyes before we began to reflect, we make light of them and ask for something beyond.

Let me briefly indicate three ways in which we who believe in Christ should be in constant enjoyment of "signs" which unite our world with the "other" world, and bring God closely into contact with our life :

1. First, we hold in our hands the Bible ; and no one can thoughtfully and devoutly read it without being sure that, however that Divine library came together, it really tells us that God was and is working in the world and in the hearts of His people. I am speaking of the Bible in a large and a broad way ; and I say that to the Christian heart it carries a message straight from God. We depreciate the evidence of the Bible because it is so familiar to us that, alas, I fear only too many of us cease to read it. But when we are perplexed by

such misgivings as I have been mentioning, we cannot read, for example, the Psalms or the Life of St. Paul without carrying away a very real assurance that God has not left Himself without witness.

2. I do not say much about the study of history at large as distinct from the Bible record of God's guidance of the life of Israel and of the early Church, because it is not very easy to speak briefly of the record, that God writes in large characters, of His direction and influence upon the lives of nations and of men.

But we each may adduce the signs of God's favour and goodness towards us from the memories of our own lives ; if only we will quicken our power of observation by that far, far too often forgotten grace of thanksgiving. Answers to prayer, if we would first pray earnestly as those who expect to be heard, and then watch for the response of our Father which is in heaven, would convince us that we have more frequent and more satisfying signs of His presence on earth and His work in our lives than we could, without experience, have claimed to be allowed to see.

3. Again, in the Sacraments, especially in the constantly renewed inward and spiritual grace of the Holy Communion, have we not—I speak reverently— a beautifully designed system just to meet the case of these distressed ones of whom we are thinking ? " A pledge to assure us "—this exactly suits their temper and their needs ; for it is a clear sign on earth, of the present reality of the heavenly power, which they are wishing were made more unmistakably vivid. I am not saying that any of us make a full and proper use of the Eucharistic Service, and that the open eyes of the heart habitually recognize it to be the very gate of heaven ; but I do say that the adherents of our Lord Jesus Christ, and not least the young, every one of them, have taken part in Holy Communions that deepen their lives in Christ in the assurance that they can so eat the flesh of Christ and drink His blood that their

sinful bodies are made clean by His body and their souls washed through His most precious blood, and that they can dwell in Christ and Christ in them.

If anyone without previous knowledge had been asked to devise some means by which timid-hearted believers in Christ, people of little intellectual skill and small knowledge of religious proofs, but characterized by real love, might have their faith in the unseen and the eternal quickened and kept bright and strong, could he have evolved any such plan as the constant recurrence of the administration of both the Sacraments of Christ's Church as they bring us to God and God to us in the very midst of earthly surroundings? In the Holy Communion we are not asked to forget earth and fly on soaring wings to heaven, and certainly we are not taking part in some mere earthly ceremony that belongs only to this world, but two worlds are ours—the bread and the wine, and the Body and Blood of Christ; heaven and earth have met and the light of heaven has shone on earth. And this we have known, and if we have known it, do we yet need any clearer sign? It is only our sinful and our cold hearts that prevent every celebration of the Holy Communion from being to us an open revelation of heaven:

> Two worlds are ours, 'tis only sin
>   Forbids us to descry
> The mystic heaven and earth within,
>   Plain as the sea and sky.

Brethren, I have finished. I do not put before you to-day any new argument, any new proofs. I merely remind you, and I remind myself of that which is already our own. God grant that we may better use the bright light which He has given us in the best of ways. Instead of asking for something more which we do not possess, instead of praying to God to make Himself from without more plain to our eyes, let us rather pray to Him to give us within the eyes that can

see, and the loving, obedient hearts to which Christ
has promised the revelation of Himself and His Father.
Our text is our prayer : " Increase our faith : Lord,
increase our faith."

*   *   *   *   *

The line of thought indicated in the preceding
sermon is followed to some extent in a sermon preached
before the University of Glasgow on January 13th,
1924. The first and last sections of this sermon may
perhaps be appropriately added here.

> " God said unto Moses, ' I am that I am.' "—Exod. iii. 14.
> " Jesus Christ the same yesterday, and to-day, and for
> ever."—Heb. xiii. 8.

THE Hebrew tenses do not correspond with those
of the English language. In the English, with our
variety of turns, we can speak with marked precision.
The Hebrew is different ; for example, one tense must
cover a larger ground of thought. But the advantage
is not all on the English side. What our English
language may gain in definiteness it loses in suggestive-
ness. It is, I think, remarkable that the Greek of the
New Testament should be matched with the Hebrew
of the Old. The Greek language is wonderfully
expressive and articulate ; the Hebrew is inclusive
without sharp-cut edges. It is sometimes half uncon-
scious of its own reach. Thus the Hebrew can compress
or comprehend what the Greek utters, and the Greek
can draw out the latent meanings of the Hebrew.

It will not, then, surprise us that two or more
different translations can be given of the Name of God,
not indeed now mentioned for the first time to Moses
but rather clearly revealed to him here, and that it
should be capable of more than one interpretation ;
for remembering the genius of the Hebrew we might
expect it to gather in more than one thought.

Some scholars have translated the NAME " I am

what I am." Those who do so think of the Everlasting
God in His abiding essence, so far as we dare to frame
such a thought. It corresponds to what we read in the
Book of Revelation of Him " Who was, and is, and is
to come." The phrase is not a mere *idem per idem*.
It is not negative, but positive ; it offers a firm ground
for our faith. In God there is nothing changeable or
alterable. He is the Alpha and the Omega, the
Almighty.

Others render the title " I will be what I will be."
But in the Hebrew this and the former translation are
not mutually exclusive. " I will be that I will be "
brings us down from the heights of heaven to God's
dealings with men.

Of God, as He is in Himself, and to Himself—I am
what I am—we can know very little. He is represented
to us equally well as dwelling in light unapproachable,
or as dwelling in the little cubic chamber of utter
darkness into which the high priest alone entered once
a year when and where only, so we are told, this holy
Name was ever pronounced by human lips. But we
observe that so far as we can and may apprehend God
as thus He is to Himself, He is the supreme personal
Object of our awe and adoration. He is not the last
effort of speculation, He is no abstract proposition.
He lives. And our intelligent worship of Him, the
Eternal Absolute, is something to affect our lives, and
is no mere ritual homage.

When we speak of God as declaring Himself under
the form " I will be that I will be," we are struck by
the appropriateness of the NAME at this particular
crisis when God was going to perform His wonders in
Egypt and to interpose in the life of His people, and
to prove that He was their own Saviour and Deliverer.
He was to touch their own experience ; He was
to make His providence mighty among them ; they
were to feel His presence about them and to adore ;
Israel and Israel's God were to meet, as faith within

corresponded to revelation without. And this was to
be continuously the case throughout the life of the
Nation. Think of the tender and strong recognitions
of this in the Psalter. God enabled His people to
extend their knowledge and appreciation of Himself
by His action among them. He enables us to do the
same. The great I AM does not Himself change ; but
we who now know Him under the name of Love see
and observe more, and ever more, of the illuminating
workings of the Eternal Love. I should, however, say
in passing that in all this matter of God's revelation of
Himself to men I believe we are wise to use very
cautiously that phrase in favourite use, " progressive
revelation," lest it should lead us to think that there
is a change on God's side as He more fully shows
Himself. The movement is, by God's grace, on man's
side, as God gives him the power to behold better and
better what was there all the time ; so shall we get rid
of the unfortunate implications of the notion that God
in early times accommodated Himself to man's imper-
fections. God is ; and He guides man's eyes to develop
their power of beholding Him more fully.

I believe then, that in this new Name, not new in
its use, but new in its claims and promises, God
declared Himself to Moses as the One God Who would
justify Himself to His people, by His actions for them
and among them, and by His taking part in their
life.

It will not serve my purpose either to trace that
action further in detail, or to study now other titles
of God or attributes assigned to Him in the Prophets,
as they called Israel to rightness of life by showing,
under other phrases, Who and What God is, what is
His relation to His people, and what is the necessary
response from a faithful people to such a God as was
theirs. I now desire to turn to the Lord Jesus Christ ;
and I make my transition as naturally or as abruptly
as the first verses of the Epistle to the Hebrews,

" God, Who at sundry times, and in divers manners spake in time past unto the fathers by the prophets, hath in these last days spoken unto us *in* His Son." I believe that the Son of God, Who declared that He that hath seen Me hath seen the Father, makes Himself known among men by the same promise " I will be that I will be." Indeed it is my aim to suggest the importance of experience in the Christian life, and that just as of old God showed Himself to Israel through a developing experience, so does Christ appeal to the experience of His disciples to-day. Such an Epiphany is His towards us now.

Those who have no faith will always say, " Prove to us first that Jesus is divine. When we see clearly with the intellect that He is God we will come to Him." But it is not the intellect alone that sways man ; there is the heart, and there is the will besides. And Christ says to us, as He said long ago, *not* " See and then come," but " Come and ye shall see." So it is still. The venture of faith must be made and it will justify itself. In the words of a great leader, " It was not by argument that God saved the world."

*   *   *   *   *

To-day, I know, much time is spent in investigating the manner and method of the Incarnation, the relation between the manhood and the Godhead of Christ. Many are ready to intrude into our Lord's consciousness as if our psychology could tell us of the composition of His unique Personality, which, because it is unique, is beyond our human power to explain. The inquiry is made, " What of Christ before His baptism ? " " What of Him afterwards ? " " What do we mean by the power of God acting through human nature ? " or, to use an older phrase, " What of Hooker's Grace of Unction ? " " What was the extent or the rule of the restriction in divine knowledge inherent in the self-emptying of deity ? " " How did the Lord Himself feel in relation to God ? " But over all such things I believe are written the words : "Such knowledge is too wonderful for me ; it is high ; I cannot attain it." "The secret things belong unto the Lord our God." It is those which are revealed that "belong unto us and to our children for ever."

Therefore, in my last words would I rather urge, in regard to anyone who is holding back from the love of God in Christ till a solution shall be found to the mystery of the Incarnation, to ask such a one simply, open-mindedly to allow the Lord Christ to prove Himself real, human, and divine, in the experience of ordinary life, with its sins waiting for forgiveness, with its puzzles that admit of no philosophical, but indeed of a religious, answer, with its yearnings for better things which cannot here be found, with its sorrows that cannot be explained but only comforted—and that by One Healing Hand, and its joys which yet are wistful all the time. For yet once again for us in our own walk through life, whether through the sea or in the wilderness, on the mountain-top or as you come to the crossing of the Jordan He will be to us, He will be what He will be.

Do you remember what Bishop Wilkinson wrote in the *Life of Archbishop Benson* ?—" Almost his last public utterance was a witness to the relation which exists between the believer and the Son of God. The Christ of our youth is unveiled to us endlessly greater, stronger to save, mightier to lead than we conceived in our young days, and we worship Him. Then begins the companionship. Between companions there are confidences, and with no companions are there surer confidences than with Him."

XIV

DOCTRINE AND THE CHURCH OF ENGLAND [1]

" Now we see through a glass, darkly."—1 Cor. xiii. 12

I ASK to-day to speak of Christian doctrine and the forms of dogma which express it, not unaware that the subject bears upon present problems. There can be no doubt of the universal appeal of the Lord Christ. Those who criticize His life and His words unfavourably are comparatively very few. When one thinks of the position which He has held among varying civilizations, in the hearts of the learned, the ignorant, the rich, the poor, the young, the old, in every country, in every age, we may without exaggeration speak of His appeal as universal. Devotion to Him is world-wide, age-wide. When we come to Christian doctrine and to the statements of it, this unanimity fails. This sad fact leads many to exclaim " Let us get back to Christ away from all dogmas and among them from the formal creeds about which the Churches dispute." That sounds well ; and yet the cry disregards simple and real facts of the situation. No thing, no person affects us but as we think of it or think of him or her. It is not Christ Himself but our response to Him that will consciously influence our lives ; I am for the moment omitting the work of Christ as the Light which lighteth every man, the Light which has ever been coming into the world, moving men towards God without their identifying the light that leads them. If, I say, we are to make any personal understanding response to Christ worth having, we must have some mind about Him, some view of Him, however little we define it ; at least we

[1] A sermon preached in the Temple Church October 30th, 1927.

108

must regard Him as genuine and His words as carrying some authority for us. We need not define that authority, no—not until we wish to give a reason for our faith and love, and until we wish to share them with others. Then we must answer for ourselves or for others the question, " What think ye of Christ ? " Any reasonable answer is the beginning of a doctrine about Him. And if our doctrine is to be coherent and communicable, it must be capable of statement. Here is the spring of dogma. Again, if the disciples of Christ are to hang together in a fellowship, they must share together some views of Christ, that is, some doctrine, and then some statement of doctrine. There could be no cohesion or common ends among persons whose ideas about Him had no gathering-point.

The doctrine of the New Testament is very little formulated. Men who together had lived with Christ had come under the same spell. They all felt it and assumed it in one another, without needing frequently to express it. But when they came to carry the good news of Christ to others, they, I repeat, must answer the questions put by new converts, and explain and define a little. Here is the beginning of the doctrine of the Church. We cannot brush it all aside as un-necessary. If believers all over the world were to be united in a Church they must have at least a common faith in the simplest aspects of their acceptance of Christ.

In the next stage this doctrine was more carefully defined as the Apostles' successors found it necessary to exclude false teaching about Christ from the fellow-ship of the believers. The first simple phrases could be used to mean different things, true or false, to different people. This possibility must be prevented, and Church dogma grew up to exclude error. For example, while the Church has no right to dogmatize for any outside its own circle as to whether Christ is God or not, it makes that a test question for all who wish to enter its brotherhood, and rightly asks that the answer shall be wholehearted and not evasive. While a simple man need not join in theological discussions, yet if he is to be baptized into Christ and join the company of His Church, then his views, so far as they go, must correspond to the facts as the Church holds them. At Lausanne a prominent divine, speaking on behalf of those who have a horror of authoritative creeds, remarked that they had need to realize how much the creedless churches owed to the Catholic creeds for the maintenance of Scriptural faith. It is beyond my purpose now to deal with obvious questions here arising, as the extent of the Church, its focus of authority, its ability to interpret the Godhead of Christ, rather presupposed than defined in the New Testament, so as to meet the thought, the needs of every age.

We must, then, I urge, have doctrine, dogma. Yes: but we are bound to recall that as we draw these lines of dogma we are trying to express eternal truths in human language, and that our instruments are unequal to our task. Every line drawn to give clearness leaves something beyond it. Christ is greater than our thoughts, our phrases, about Him. There will always be something far, far above them, above our ken, before which we can only bow our heads. Our thoughts and our expression of our thoughts in formulated doctrine are only approximations towards the realities which they half hide and half disclose. They are provisional. Our forms are not decisive with the sharp precision of some clear-cut exhaustive definition. " Now we see through a glass, darkly."

And more, the very framing and the forming of the dogma are a part of a progressive effort. People are now speaking about emphasizing this or that aspect of doctrine, as if the doctrine was so securely and satisfactorily expressed in our words that we could stress it here or stress it there and yet leave the doctrine unaltered. But the balance of our phrasing marks a stage, a degree in our success.

Emphasis is not something that can, as it were, be added to or withdrawn from our completed fixed expression of doctrine ; it is a process in the execution of our attempt to present the inexpressible. Emphasis is all-important in the proportion of faith. To enlarge one feature in the portrait of an individual, to exaggerate it or to reduce it, will alter the likeness ; we too are only handling pictures.

Now permit me to make a few observations on such Christian doctrine.

First, it is a doctrine of God and therefore is not only intellectual but it must always be spiritual, and bring us into some moral relation with God. Doctrine, the statement of doctrine, dogma, are necessary to educate, to guide, to unite, to defend Christ's disciples. But all the time we want to reach to Him to Whom these things point us, to God in Christ. Since our phrases cannot carry us all the way, their value is to lead us to apprehend Him with the eyes of the soul. " The catholic faith is this : that we worship "—not that we systematize our beliefs, but that we worship God ; and service is a part and a test of worship.

The heathen, who " bow down to wood and stone " (Is. xliv. 9, 17), localize their god as if He were one of themselves, only greater, an external power with whom they have no inward association. This reduces the moral effect of their belief to a minimum. They do not understand our Lord's words, " The Kingdom of God is within you." We too must take care that our thought of God does not become similarly external, divorced from life. Such risk becomes greater when we begin to draw inferences from these our tentative statements, treating them as axioms or things proved in mathematics or science, as if we knew all the facts, and as if the infinite quality of God made no difference in our argument.

We need to think of these cautions in the great Sacrament of the Holy Communion. Our faith here, as always, has in it an element of mystery and awe, which is of course an element not of weakness but strength. It is easy here to be over-wise, over-clear in the terms which we employ, to exclaim with a confident exactitude, " Lo, here is Christ, or there," to circumscribe the eternal with the temporal. In this feast of fellowship we seek union with Christ, union with one another in Him, but a union not physical but moral, not local but heavenly, not mechanical but spiritual.

Next behold the wisdom of the Church of England which constantly requires that its doctrine should be tested by Holy Scripture. Little has been said about the truth of Scripture in recent discussions of the Prayer Book, which have chiefly ranged over prospects of settlement and ranges of toleration. Settlement is a great thing if it can be had in fact and in heart, and is not to be disturbed immediately by fresh demands and refusals, if all parties to it are able and eager to fulfil the obligations which it imposes. Toleration is also a fine thing if it does not involve a lack of convinced cohesion and does not mean that our forces are on paper united against God's enemies and in fact divided. The appeal to Scripture has not been very strong. Perhaps people feel upon less safe ground now than of old when they turn to Scripture, for science, physical and historical, has led to fresh views of some aspects of the Bible, and many do not recognize that this does not touch the cogency of its spiritual message, and that it is the frame and not the picture which has been altered. There is no time to pursue this subject ; one thing, however, must be clear to those who believe in the Christian revelation, namely, that those who lived in Christ's company, those who had been specially trained by Him personally or knew those who had this privilege, those upon whom the

Holy Spirit first came, must have had an insight into heavenly things and eternal truths to which no subsequent age, however inspired and gifted, can pretend. Quite plainly, we are right to test our doctrines by the utterances of such great teachers, and whatever may be the weakness of our texts or of the memories of those who reported Christ's words, still in the New Testament we have the surest guide in stating and testing our doctrines.

Lastly, while the acute mind has its place, and learning and study are all-important, this question of doctrine is not a matter for the theological expert alone. If Church doctrine is a spiritual and moral and Christian thing, then all men can claim some grasp of it; indeed they have a responsibility which they cannot entirely pass on to the technical scholar. That is one side of the matter. The other side is that if each has his place in estimating the doctrine, he must remember the best qualification for so doing laid down by our Lord. " If any man makes it his will to do the will of God, he shall know about the doctrine." The quiet discharge by a Christian man of his duty fits him better than anything else for judging of the doctrine, the teaching of God, as a humble seeker after the truth. And duty does not mean only public and personal duty done before men, but duty reverenced in those secret places of the life, the purpose and the thought which are only open to the eye of God. " Blessed are the pure in heart for they—they shall see God." The secret of doctrine, the secret of life, of life in Christ is theirs.

XV

TRUTH AND SYMBOL [1]

"The hope which is laid up for you in heaven."—Col. i. 5

IT is likely that the anniversary of Armistice Day
has quickened again the sense of loss in the hearts
of those whose dearest laid down their lives in the War.
On the day itself two years ago I well remember how
the sense of relief, the thought that our armies were
soon to be free to return, made us think the more of
those who would never come back. There were many
who in all their true sympathy with those who were
preparing a welcome for their husbands and brothers
and friends, by contrast felt once more their own grief
and desolation, as acutely as when the first news had
arrived, perhaps years before, that the form which
they loved so tenderly would abide for ever in a
soldier's grave in a far land.

Two years have passed since that time, and during
those two years we know of not a few who have tried
to get into touch with those whom they love, and to
peep behind the veil, that very thin veil which divides
this life from the Beyond. Such persons have probably
found the comfort of friends unsatisfactory or conventional. Perhaps their friends have spoken to them
in the words of Holy Scripture; and this language has
sounded unreal: it appeared to place those for whom
they mourn in a state or environment that makes no
appeal; to represent them as engaged in occupations
which seem wholly foreign to their character as they
knew it; indeed, to be so far removed from the
general scope and aspirations of their own lives as to
be worth nothing, either for comfort or for meditation,
as they have asked themselves the question: " Where

[1] A Sermon preached in St. Margaret's, Westminster, November
14th, 1920.

is he ? What is he doing now ? Can he see me ? Does he feel for me ? Does he miss me ? " I doubt not that there are some who in a revulsion of feeling from comfortless consolations have discarded the words of Holy Scripture and have sought other methods which seem to promise some clearer understanding and intercourse to bring them near to those whom they miss, day by day, in an aching void.

It is not my intention this morning to develop the doctrine, the full comfort, and joy and truth of the last two words which were added to the Apostles' Creed, and, though it was in the second century, and early in it, that the Creed on the whole took its present shape, did not secure their place in it until the eighth century—" *sanctorum communionem.*" I believe that there is a Communion of Saints. It is indeed this Communion founded in Christ which is the real bridge between the world before our eyes and the world that is at present hidden from our gaze ; and it is in these words that we have rightly to seek the strength of the unseen, but lasting, comradeship of those whom we love and have lost.

But I rather ask to-day to speak of the unfortunate way in which the words of the Bible as they stand, the phrases supposed to comfort mourners, have been misunderstood, so that the real truths which they put before us are changed into forms of thought which are altogether unsatisfying. This, I believe, is to a large extent due to a confusion of thought caused by the symbolic shape in which the facts of the other world are portrayed ; and it may be worth our while, especially in view of recent discussions, briefly to inquire what is the value and what is the place of symbolism in the Holy Scriptures.

We may answer that there are certain truths that are important for us to know, which can only be presented to our present powers through the use of symbols and pictures. If things which are wholly without the range

of our present experience and of our very faculties are
to be brought in any degree within our ken, it can
only be done by translating them into pictures, which
symbolize, but do not reproduce or describe or define,
the things themselves. And when our finite minds
are directed to the infinite or to human nature in a
new or in a glorified state, such a form of representation, I presume, is not just one means out of many by
which the truths of another world could have been
brought within our grasp ; as we are situated, it is the
only way by which they could touch our minds and
hearts. God is not hiding the things of a new order
from us ; it is that we have no powers directly to
apprehend the things themselves.

If I am correct, one or two conclusions will follow.
In the first place, we must not say that for this reason
uncertainty or unreality attaches to the mysteries
revealed to us. Just as the facts of past history now
reach us through the record which describes them, so
the facts of the eternal world actually reach us through
the symbols which represent them. It is no use for
us to try to pierce through the symbolism as if we could
thus get some clearer knowledge of the beyond. For
us, as in the old Greek story, the curtain is the picture :
the symbol itself, better than anything else, brings the
realities to our minds.

I do not deny that it will remove difficulties here
and there for us to be aware that we are dealing with
a representation of realities, and not with the realities
themselves. For then, for example, we will not make
the mistake of demanding that one picture of the other
world should accurately correspond with every other
picture, or press the details in an unintelligent literal-
ism. Nor shall we reject the underlying ideas because
others before us have wrongly insisted that these
outward details marked out the exact truth ; we can
still, with corrected vision, learn something even in
the Campo Santo in Pisa. It is a loss and not a gain

if, through following the line of a criticism, which may rightly assure us that the facts, when we can know them, will be different from the figures, we are led to ignore the figures and to say that they have no substance behind them and offer no firm ground for faith, and hope, and sure expectation. The figures themselves, I repeat, are clear and true to us ; we cannot get to the other side of them. And no words of any kind can compass the whole truth, still less circumscribe it. This is the case with truths that are within our present human experience ; but it is much more fully the case when we are speaking of the verities of another world.

I feel little doubt that some of us miss the richness of the meaning of the Bible through an attempt to explain, which often means to explain away, the pictorial words which it employs upon eternal truths.

What I have been saying, I believe, has its place in guiding our efforts to grasp the life of those who have already passed into the other world, and to understand the hope which is laid up for us in Heaven.

We read, for example, the great visions in the Book of the Revelation, and frame our notions of Heaven from their splendid representations. But some, instinctively feeling that a city of pure gold, like unto clear glass, cannot be reality, pass the whole thing by —the representation and the thing represented—as sheer foolishness. And the flippant members of such a section mock at the Christian faith which, to their shallow fancy, seems condemned just because they stupidly take its poetry for prose. Others accept the words more reverently, but still regard them as only a figment of poetic imagination. Symbolical to them means unsubstantial, unreal, untrue. Some, again, while they cannot imagine that a city whose length and breadth and height are all equal, is presented as an accurate description, nevertheless, inconsistently, in some part still confuse the symbol with the reality, and, pressing the details of the picture, imagine that the life of Heaven will consist of an everlasting and idle song of praise.   Clarity and continuity of thought are required, lest having recognized that our terms are not definitions we should use them as if they were.

And there are those who are apt to think of the life immediately after death as being accurately described in the common expressions which we are bound to employ in speaking of something that is quite unknown to us.   To them the words " rest and peace " mean idleness, and a life from which all interest has been banished.   Their ideas of the state to which those whom they love have passed corresponds more closely than they know to the Jewish conception of Sheol as a state far removed from the gladness of serving God and from the consciousness of His invigorating Presence.

Such thoughts as these result in real disaster.   They dim our hopes of the world to come.   They rob us of our consolation when our friends pass away ;   they make us think poorly of Our Lord's return :   they make us cling to this life from a fear of the unknown, from which these mistaken thoughts have already taught us to shrink.   There are indeed those who could not understand the words of St. Paul when he said that it was very far better to see no more of his old friends at Philippi and to depart and to be with Christ, for they would far sooner be at home in Philippi than newly come to Paradise or be ever with the Lord in Heaven.

This life seems large and rich and interesting, and, on the other hand, the life of the world to come looks pale, colourless, monotonous, unsubstantial, lacking in human association, artificial, and unspontaneous.

The gospel story of Our Lord first passing into Paradise and then restored to His sorrowing disciples, slow to believe good news that seemed too good to be true, should teach us better than this.   The history of the penitent thief, to go no further, as we reverently contemplate together the Forgiver and the forgiven, assures us that in Paradise the Lord and he were living through death ; and if the Lord was living, we know that He must have been doing. In the sorrow of these times, when the career of many good, young, active Christian men has been brought to a sudden close, I have comforted myself by remembering that they were called away from service here because they, perhaps the very best, were already wanted for higher work and grander activities elsewhere. They had received promotion. And then the Risen Christ abolished death and brought life and incorruption to light : " for now is Christ risen from the dead, the first fruits of them that slept." We read of the glorious change that has passed upon Him, that He was no longer bound by the spatial and other limitations of the life we here know with our present faculties. He could appear as He pleased, and go as He pleased, without the check of distance or of barred doors. His voice could be unfamiliar to His friends, His very companionship need not disclose Him ; He was changed, yet He was still the same, the same in look, in love and strength, in power, in lovableness ; as He taught them the hearts of His disciples burned within them as of old ; as the tones of His voice once more spoke her name, Mary fell at His feet ; the doubting Thomas learned, what his feeble test could never have guaranteed, the grand truth that from the grave was given back to the disciples the Master Whom they loved, now recognized first by him, the first sceptic, as his Lord and his God, never to die again, living for evermore.

Here is no picture, no fancy ; here we behold a life which, while it does not discard its earthly association, yet belongs to another order, spiritual and real. And here we catch a glimpse even on earth, not in symbol but in fact, of a similar change which awaits us when the body of our humiliation is conformed to the body of His glory and we come to the glad day when there shall be no more curse, and His servants shall serve Him and they shall see His face, and God shall wipe away all tears from their eyes.

The prize is indeed great and the contest grand, through the power of the Holy Spirit to be made worthy of the things which God hath prepared for them that love Him. " Beloved, now are we the sons of God, and it doth not yet appear what we shall be ; but we know that when He shall appear, we shall be like Him ; for we shall see Him as He is. And mark you—every man that hath this hope in Him purifieth himself, even as He is pure."

XVI

CHURCH ORDER AND DOCTRINE [1]

"The liberty of the glory of the children of God."—Rom. viii. 21

WHEN last I had the honour of preaching before the University I tried to lift up our thoughts to the ascended Christ. Now I ask to carry them one step farther, to the coming of the Holy Spirit. . . .

The Holy Spirit is one with Christ, and He reveals the way and the will of Christ Himself, just as Christ revealed the Father in the terms of human life. If we bear this in mind, a clear authority, a personal sympathy, a direct understanding, something more decisive than a vague influence is seen to belong to the guidance of the Spirit upon apostolic utterance and apostolic procedure. . . . Christ meant all the working of the Holy Spirit to be the most real thing in the world after He had left it. . . .

There are some who will interest themselves in the facts of Christ's life on earth, but the range of their apprehension ceases at His death. They dismiss the Resurrection from their thoughts. The Apostles began with it. Their speeches and letters do not dwell in much detail upon the incidents of Christ's ministry. The Holy Spirit taught them that it was only after the Ascension of Christ that the full gospel opened. To tell their hearers all about the life of Christ here in this world would have been a retrospect, and they would have been speaking about something in which their converts had no share at first hand. The gospel which they did preach was the gospel of the Living Christ now working, without the limitations belonging to His sojourn among men, working by the Spirit in the heart and in the careers of every fresh disciple who joined the fast-growing company of the Christian Church. . . .

[1] A sermon preached in the Cathedral Church of Durham November 16th, 1930, before the University of Durham.

It was the Holy Spirit who taught the Apostles what to say about Christ, and made real to those who listened the things of Christ. Christ will always be outside us (just a person to study and to read about) until the Holy Spirit leads each of us to say, as we look up into His face with the eye of faith, " *My* Lord and *my* God." The Holy Spirit makes everything personal, vivid, and real. We need to-day a fuller belief in this real and gracious work of the Holy Spirit as He brings God near to us.

And also, I go on to say, we need a fuller belief in the freedom of His work. In Christ Himself there was, in the noblest sense, something totally unconventional. It is so in the stirrings of the Spirit Who continues Christ's work, Who makes the true extension of the Incarnation. Christ surprised His contemporaries by the freshness of His manner and His words. He did not teach them as the scribes. He was no traditionalist. He saw things under the guise of eternity. Rules and regulations about the Sabbath, or the washings, or the code of respectability had no weight with Him. It was not the schemes and systems of men, but the will of His Father which counted. I suppose, then, we might *expect* something of the same in the Holy Spirit's movements ; and as a matter of fact we find the same freshness in them.

For proof, once more look back to those early days, and see how He surprised the Apostles with the things He did and the truths He taught. The day of Pentecost itself, as it actually came about, was, I imagine, a great surprise. Think, too, of the astonishment when St. Peter was told not to call things and persons common and unclean where his whole religion had so far taught him to use these terms. How wonderful that the Holy Spirit should fall upon an outsider like Cornelius even before he was baptized. Recall the modern freshness of St. Paul, who broke away from Jewish tradition and declared that " where the Spirit of the Lord is, there is liberty." All these and many other such things worketh the selfsame spirit, free as the wind itself, to use the comparison our Lord employed in His talk with Nicodemus.

Let me this morning call to your special attention two aspects of the Spirit's freedom during those first days. I refer to organization and doctrine.

We look at the Church's ministry, and we find scholars still discussing what bishops and presbyters really were. Do the terms mainly emphasize offices or officers ? Do they lay the stress upon the functions to be discharged or the isolating commission of those who were to discharge them ? And what was the succession of those who came after ? Were they like a new series of trustees for the one faith, filling the place of those who had gone before, or did they succeed by a strict line of descent, to which was attached the grace of the Holy Spirit ? Who shall ever say at what moment St. Paul received his authorization ? The Holy Spirit did not, so it seems, from the beginning initiate at once and suddenly a fixed and conclusive system.

There is also a freedom in the expression of Christian Truth. The doctrinal statements of the Apostles follow no method. The cardinal account of the institution of the Holy Communion only comes incidentally in St. Paul's letter—and that because of some irreverence at Corinth. If it had not been for pushing people at Philippi we should never have had the superb and stupendous statement—even so, not a definition—of the sevenfold humiliations of Him as Man, Who existed before all time as God.

I am not one of those who say, " Let us get back to Christ ; what does He say about organization, what does He say about Creeds ? " Very little, no doubt ; but He left a common love and a fellowship behind Him, and a fellowship cannot extend without some formulation. The company of believers must be united first by their love to the Lord ; but also according to His own ordinance by the social Sacraments of joint membership in Christ and of joint participation of His Body and Blood, and further by a common expression of their loyalty to Him. And I do not shrink from the later *precision* of our creeds ; I believe they are a part of the work of the Holy Spirit Who, as Christ promised, guides us into all the truth. As errors crept in, it became necessary to exclude them, though there is no real advance in the elaborated Creed of the service of Holy Communion from the simpler Creed in Morning Prayer. It only makes it more difficult to misinterpret or misunderstand the terms of the shorter form which implies just the same. But in the earliest days it was Christ Himself—His Being still undefined in set terms—Christ, their Living Lord, Who filled the hearts and minds of His disciples ; Christ, as the Holy Spirit interpreted Him to them. And in our own day we have to be careful lest a right interest in the accuracy of intellectual definitions should replace and displace the Living Christ in our own hearts and lives. We too need in our attitude to God the glad liberty of those first days of the out-pouring of the Holy Spirit.

We must see to it that we do not in any respect lose this sense of freedom. We thankfully acknowledge the due order which has been developed under the guidance of the Holy Spirit, in Church organization and in the Church's teaching. We are not to act as if we were pioneers in a new country, without any real help from the experience of previous travellers to guide our steps. Yet we have to be on our guard lest we should fix all our attention upon the machinery of system, or again upon the forms of creeds, and lest we fail to catch the vision of the Holy Spirit Himself behind it all. The channels which He has cut are intended to further and not to hinder or to cramp the distribution of the water of life.

There are other happenings to-day which must lead

us to emphasize these two so great things, the reality and the freedom of the Holy Spirit's work. Let me illustrate in one or two ways. There are some who, wishing to be rid of any creed, speak as if Christian ethics were an elaborated scheme of conduct or of moral philosophy which, once formed, could stand on its own foundation apart from any continuing faith in Christ. For the Christian, ethics mean a growing interpretation of life and of its opportunities in the light of the Holy Spirit's revelation of the mind of Christ. He thus gives them reality and firmness. For the Christian the belief in goodness, the hope of progress, rests upon his Faith in the Risen Christ and upon the Holy Spirit Who lights our way to Him. " If Christ be not risen, then is our preaching vain."

Others are revolting from the Christian standard because they do not like it and declare that it has no stability or reality in it. We Christians must oppose this view, but we must be careful that in maintaining the *reality* of what the Holy Spirit has built up we still do not ignore the *freedom* of His movements. Sometimes the revolt *may* be from prohibitions and dictates which have lost their savour and become unreal, rigid, and cold because the free living breath of the Holy Spirit no longer animates them. However good its results may be or may have been, human authority, with Christ now omitted, does not appeal, nor do laws of right conduct received at second-hand. To carry weight, these laws must be received from Christ Himself personally endorsing the experience of the past for the present use. And this comes from the movement of the Holy Spirit.

Turning to another direction we may observe, once more, that it is much more difficult to keep in real and vital contact with Christ through the Holy Spirit than to carry on regular acts of devotion and to follow Church conventions ; we can make more of the external forms and of what I may (by a paradox) call

the statistics of worship, than of the life which is
" hid with Christ in God." We of the clergy have
constantly to be on our guard lest our own professionalism lead us into an unreality which will quickly
be matched by a spiritless externalism on the part of
our people. We have, yes, in the name of reality, we
have to call ourselves and to call them back to the
Holy Spirit, ever fresh and invigorating. It is He who
can bring the power of stirring, radiant life to our
creeds and prayers and rites, and give to them a
glowing consciousness of reality. When we say that
the world does not want our Christ, are we sure we
are not presenting to it a Christ of memory and past
history, or showing to it a conventional Christianity
stronger in phrase and form than in its spiritual
reality and freedom ?

May God, then, make us bold to-day to mean just
what we say when we say, " I believe in the Holy
Ghost." I believe in Him as the Lord, I believe in
Him as the Giver of Life : Life real and young and free.
That is a faith which can win the world for the Divine
Christ. Here is the glorious liberty of God's children.
And I believe—and I may say so in preaching to this
congregation—that the young men and the young
women have as great a part as we have who are older,
in bringing this faith in the Holy Spirit of God to bear
upon the worship and the work of our country and
empire to-day. Christ was a young man when He
lived and when He died, little older than many of the
students in this great University. He certainly belongs
at least as much to the younger generation as to the
older ; and if I have been right in what I have said
about the guidance of the Holy Spirit, as He reveals
the mind of Christ, it is the young, to whom their own
life is real and fresh, that are specially called to listen
to what He has to say, not to us who are older, but to
themselves, about this liberty of the glory of the
children of God.

PART IV
WORSHIP

XVII

TRUE WORSHIP AND THE ENGLISH LAITY [1]

" God is Spirit; and they that worship him must worship in spirit and truth."—John iv. 24 (R.V.)

IF we had planned the details of our Lord's short sojourn among men our scheme would have been very different from that which was His own will and choice. When the time was so short we should not have allotted thirty years out of thirty-three to preparation, reserving only three years for the actual ministry, its progress and its close. And if we had learnt that there were only three years available we should not have arranged that they should be spent as they were. Certainly we would not have found place for His more private occupations. We should have approved of the Sermon on the Mount and all that He said and did when great multitudes followed Him. To the hours spent in the great teachings in the Temple which marked the closing week of His life we should have raised no objection, nor to the special education of His Apostles and His last discourses to them. Such a mighty miracle as the raising of Lazarus would have matched our purpose, for though performed on one man, it was bound to have far-reaching results.

But we should not have provided time for His talks with individuals and for the personal attention which He gave to people one by one. We should have said that this kind of detailed work must be left over till afterwards, to be carried out by His disciples after He had gone, that His own days could be better spent,

[1] A sermon preached in St. Dunstan's in the West, Fleet Street, May 10th, 1927, at the annual service of the National Church League.

and more fruitfully, if He gave Himself wholly to mass meetings and to public utterances. The blessing of the little children we should have admitted ; the parables, even those heard by a few, and every detail of the Passion, however particular. But we should have ruled out the talk with Nicodemus, the notice of Zacchæus, the story of the woman who was a sinner, the conversation with the young ruler, and similar sayings. These things would have been too small and too personal for our notion of a grand mission.

Yet, when we come to look deeper, I think we shall find that some of the most arresting acts and sayings of Christ were done or spoken in the more private manner. The personal appeal which belonged to the original incident has made also a personal appeal to millions and millions of people through sixty generations of Christians.

Plainly all this is true in regard to the story of the woman of Samaria, from which my text is taken. Here not only might we have thought that there was no occasion for the Lord to enter into conversation with one woman ; but we should further have thought that she was an unpromising person to receive His blessed address. Again, we should have anticipated that if He was to speak to her at all, He would confine Himself to such topics as sin, repentance, and improvement. Least of all should we have expected that to this woman of all the inhabitants of Palestine, He would in a private talk have entrusted the revelation of the great principles of worship. No doubt, she gave Him an opening. Like many others she was interested in the religious agitations of her time. She knew something about the rivalry and disputes of the Jews and the Samaritans in regard to the correct worship of God. As soon as she saw that she was in the company of a prophet, she thought that she would seize the opportunity to get an authoritative opinion upon the matter under discussion. But even so, in spite of the special opportunity which the woman's question opened, it does still stand as a marvel of the Divine wisdom and insight that such a woman was the first to hear the glorious words of my text.

Our Lord, as was His way, did not reply to the little question which the woman put to Him. He lifted it up on to a higher level, and disclosed something of the much wider and more important truths to which the limited question was but distantly related. It was in a similar manner that a futile question, " Who is my neighbour ? " evoked one of the most beautiful parables which from the other side of neighbourliness educated the inquirer and all those who listened to it, in the principles of Christian service. In the same way, as we remember now in these Great Forty Days, He diverted the last inquiry of the Apostles before His Ascension from an idle speculation into the challenge of a world-wide witness. So here. Worship is revealed to be not some earthly obligation concerning the proper place of which partisans and extremists may dispute. Men will always make mistakes about it if they turn their eyes to the earth. Worship that is genuine worship starts with God. It is an attitude of the spirit, and its inspiration is truth. Finally and supremely it is in Christ Himself we find the true object of worship, for it is He Who once for all has revealed the Father, and also through Christ Himself it is that our own spirits have access to worship God ; we rightly end our prayers with the words " through Jesus Christ Our Lord."

We may go on to say that Our Lord in entrusting this open secret of worship to this woman of Samaria testifies to a fact which some of us may have observed, though many more might be inclined to discredit it. I firmly believe that, as was the case with this woman, so there are numbers who might have been considered only to possess such a limited apprehension of spiritual things as to be incapable of grasping anything but the most elementary lessons, and yet in practice and experience have shown themselves quite equal to enter with heavenly profit into serious doctrinal issues.

Let me offer you three illustrations ; the first from my experience as a schoolmaster, the second from what I have observed as a bishop, the third drawn from the testimony of others in the Foreign Mission field.

(1) When I was a schoolmaster, year by year in my preparation of a hundred candidates for Confirmation, I was surprised to note the eager way in which boys of fifteen years old would drink in an exposition of sacramental truth.

(2) One scene as a bishop I always treasure. I was giving my Confirmation Charge in a tiny village church filled to overflowing with some of the little people crowding up to my very chair. I was facing the Saxon tower, which itself gave testimony to the many generations through which the truth as it is in Jesus had been the inspiration of the lives of the little community. I spoke of the Body and Blood of Christ verily and indeed taken and received by the faithful in the Lord's Supper. I hesitated to develop the subject very deeply, and yet the silence and the rapt attention of the children urged me to go forward, and I went on to speak very fully of this Divine mystery. Now I never hesitate to discuss such things in simple language.

(3) The missionaries inform us that uneducated converts are, nevertheless, able to appreciate the deeper realities which the Holy Spirit has to teach them of the things of God. This illuminating guidance of the Lord, these observations of my own which others must share, this witness from far lands, all unite to show us that God has revealed Himself to babes, and that those who are destitute of the wisdom of this world need not, to use St. Paul's words, be " foolish " or unable to bring an understanding mind to bear upon what God has revealed to men through Jesus Christ Our Lord. Creed and worship, praying and believing,

are not matters in which we are wholly dependent upon the expert and the professor of theology and liturgiology. Before now, God has used the foolish things of the world and the weak things of the world and things which are despised, for His purposes, that they may be fulfilled in Christ Jesus, Who was made unto us wisdom from God and righteousness and sanctification and redemption.

These last great words support what I have been saying from yet another and a practical angle. We are made the more sure that humble folk can discern and rightly judge of spiritual truth in their hearts, when we observe its unquestionable results as displayed in their lives. Alas! we doubt the redeeming power of Christ, His power to redeem fallen men, not only from the guilt of their sin, but from its hold upon their lives. But the Bible pages from first to last show us how the might of God's grace can divert the whole current of a life, out of weakness can make men strong, can transform the sinner into the saint, and transfigure the chief of sinners into the prince of missionaries. Our own efforts in trying to reclaim the weak and the lost would be stronger and more successful if we had a more lively faith in the divine sovereignty of Him Who came to seek them and to save them. " They say all miracles are past." This is not so, and the miracle of the changed life would be witnessed more frequently if we really believed that Christ's power rests upon us, that, following His example, we too may be the agents in casting out the devils of sin in their many hideous forms.

At this time, however, I am not so much thinking of the way in which unlikely people are able to reach to the heights of goodness, but I return to the consideration of the way in which plain folk are able to judge of spiritual verities. I do not pretend that I have not broached this special subject of worship in spirit and truth with a definite reference to the subject of the new

Prayer Book which is exercising the minds of us all. Now the cry is raised about us, " Trust the expert." " What right have ordinary folk to question the decisions of the learned about the right and the wrong in worship ? " " Follow the direction of the doctrinal specialist as he sits in his study." " Take your lead from the priest as he stands before the altar." This morning I am urging that the humble and devout Christian, the unprofessional Churchman, the man in the pew, is fully entitled to have his own opinion and to express it. By an instinct of " sanctified common sense " simple people often go to the heart of a matter. I believe these inexpert worshippers can, through what Bishop Westcott called "the logic of the soul," offer a judgment, well worthy to be regarded, as to whether this or that practice or teaching is able to justify itself as a part of English devotion and has a right to claim a place in the public worship of the English Church and nation.

The ordinary member of a congregation cannot entirely leave these things to an official determination ; in England, at any rate, he is bound to think for himself. Official decisions pronounced by weighty persons and serious bodies count for much. We must educate our minds by such decisions and thoughts of others ; we cannot act as if we were the first men in the world to be faced by the problems which confront us ; we cannot discuss the principles of worship as if we were excursionists in the field of faith and doctrine and needed no guides and might discard all experience which is not our own. Nevertheless, we cannot surrender the sacred trust of our own consciences into the keeping of others, however august they may be, nor can we, without intelligent inquiry, regard ourselves as relentlessly tied by formal resolutions, however duly and dutifully ratified. And indeed when we *are* seeking guides we dare not limit ourselves to the guides of the moment, nor, among them, exclusively to those who beckon to us imperiously to plant our feet in their own footmarks. We must also be sensitive to catch the echoes from the past, in some cases, it may be, echoes of warning ; and we must, in determining our own course, still estimate at their right value the words which go on sounding from wise and loyal men who, outwardly parted from us but still near to us in the Communion of the saints, now are enjoying the nearer vision of the Truth. We want to lift up our hearts towards them as they worship now. We want to be sure that we lift up our hearts to the Lord, their Lord and ours. In His presence there is a clear call to charity, and no one must let his taste in worship interfere with the enjoyment of others when in matters of free choice they naturally wish to follow their own tastes in prayer and praise. But in Christ's presence there is no place for expediency if it is contrasted with truth ; there is no right to acquiesce in " strange doctrines," not agreeable to the Holy Scriptures, because others feel comfort in them: Our Lord's life was a constant protest against those who derived great delight from religious error. In His presence we may not surrender principle for peace, especially when peace is likely enough to be " peaceless peace " if bought at such a price.

We cannot, I urge, divest ourselves of our own responsibility in regard to the way in which we bow to authority ; that is not an English way of life or of freedom or of worship. I am well aware that in these days, among the fluctuating inconsistencies and the self-contradictions of others, I myself am almost required to apologize for keeping one steady course. But I repeat that, paying all due respect to the important views of important men, whether vacillating or steady, we dare not stand aside in silence, if, after carefully weighing the matter, we reach the conclusion that they are wrong ; we dare not wash our hands of our own duty. I know the temptation to do so is very great.   It has indeed pressed heavily upon me.   But I have a larger loyalty than to follow colleagues, however respected, or numbers, however eminent, a primary duty to my own conscience, to the truth as I humbly try to see it, to Him Who is the Truth, as I attempt to lift up my poor eyes to see His Face :

> This above all : to thine own self be true,
> And it must follow, as the day the night,
> Thou canst not then be false to any man.

The truth !   Worship in truth !   Yes, and worship in spirit and truth !   Here we touch the subjective side of worship and we are fenced from regarding the objective side too highly and out of proportion.   The objective side is obviously and, of course, of supreme importance.   Who in this life could venture to contemplate worship without its recurrent day of weekly prayer and praise, without its churches, without its fixed times of private devotion and Bible study, without its outward sacraments conveying their inward grace, without its Book of Common Prayer ?   But it is possible to sacrifice the inward to the outward, and the inward is the more important.   Do we not read that in the Holy City there is no temple since none is there needed for worship in the Divine presence ?   " The Lord God Almighty and the Lamb are the temple of it." The new Prayer Book, I fear, tends to exaggerate the outward and to desert the inward.   Specially look at the service of the Holy Communion ;   the maintenance of the one service subjectively touches, to my thinking, a deeper truth of unity, a deeper *spirit* of fellowship, than the provision of two liturgies expected to conciliate two parties ranged externally into two outward schools. So also, while the Lord Himself is truly and in deed brought to our inmost selves through effective signs in this His own service, yet must we ever be careful lest the outward should cease to be the channel for receiving by faith the inward Food and, approached independently of its inner use, become the object of an external worship, public or private. The compromise which you are aware that I have steadily pressed in regard to the New Prayer Book would exclude what I regard as the error of two services of Holy Communion and the dangers connected with Reservation.

Spirit and truth ! Indeed they are hard to pursue, hard to gain, and hard to make the standard of our worship. It is so easy to ignore the teaching of the Epistle to the Colossians and to find our satisfaction in outward things which come within our own limited speech and touch and range. It is sadly easy to follow the mere customs of others, to follow rules, to rely on ordinances, to think we are worshipping the Father when we champion Jerusalem or are the partisans of Gerizim. But if we are really risen with Christ we shall long to learn in our worship simply and whole-heartedly to seek the things that are above, we shall love the things of the spirit and humbly desire just to be the disciples, it may be the suffering disciples, of the truth. " The Father seeketh *such* to worship Him." Oh, may He purify our hearts and cleanse our vision and make us not wholly unworthy to be ranked among that number !

XVIII

ART AND ETERNAL BEAUTY [1]

"For glory and for beauty."—Exod. xxviii. 2

THE people of Norfolk and Norwich strongly feel the kinship between themselves and their county and city ; and it is natural that the memory of a great Norwich man, whose work specially dealt with subjects dear to the hearts of his fellow-citizens alike a hundred years ago and to-day, should be receiving so hearty and cordial a tribute. This morning we are met before God in the church which is identified with his burial ; and we ask not only to look back respectfully to the date, a century ago, when the eyes and the hand which had wrought so wonderfully rested from their labour, but also in our thanksgiving to lift up our hearts heavenward in these celebrations. It is wise that festivals of this kind should be held a hundred years after the death of the eminent man whose fame they honour. When the centenary of a man's birth is made much of there are many men still living who knew him well. The force of his personality has been too recent to allow of the calm and detached and sure attitude with which we to-day are able to think of our hero. By the lapse of years judgments are mellowed, differences are stilled, and the future generation can speak with a greater unanimity and far more certainty than a man's own contemporaries.

I need not say this morning that it is no intention of mine to speak of John Crome as those speak of him who are experts in the matter of his work and in regard to the Norwich school of painters as a whole. In their writings and their speeches they have *placed* him, so

[1] A sermon preached in St. George's Colegate, Norwich, April 22nd, 1921, at the celebration of the Crome Centenary.

to speak, and by their criticisms have taught those
who wish to learn where to look for the characteristics
of his art, to appreciate his execution, and to reach to
the nature of the genius behind. To-day it is rather
my privilege to speak of the work of this and other
artists on its eternal side. And indeed those who
know tell us that it is the touch of the eternal in his
pictures that is Crome's own glory.

We must all have felt something greater than ourselves or our world, something that lifts our hearts to
a fairer and grander Beyond, when we have stood in
the presence of something superbly beautiful. There
is a radiance in the opening of the spring morning in
our Norfolk country in this wonderful season ; there
is a solemnity in the glory of a rich and glowing sunset.
We are lifted above ourselves by the splendid greatness
and finish of noble architecture, and by the tones of
music tender or sublime. Thoughts " too deep for
tears " are often stirred in the hearts of men by works
of nature or man's craft, which appeal to us by their
exquisite charm ; or again both the living human form
seen at its loveliest or portrayed in sculpture and
painting touches us with a sweet and soul-stirring
delight. There are some of us whom an unself-
conscious distinction of face or form will always
enchant. Who can have strayed in the Vatican
galleries or the museum in Naples, unmoved ? Is it
that such wonderful visions, lifted far above the scenes
and sights of " common day," point those who have
eyes to see and devout hearts to wonder, point them
forward to the glories of the celestial country with

> Its happy, holy portion
>   Refection for the blest
> True vision of true beauty
>   The cure of all distrest.
> Where all the halls of Sion
>   For aye shall be complete,
> And in the land of beauty
>   All things of beauty meet.

And do not let anyone suppose that here and now the true art that sets forth true Beauty may be rightly disengaged from its heavenly focus or separated from the blessing of the Church. For the Church of Christ, if it is true to its high calling, not only has a welcome for art and artist but is able to consecrate their power and appeal. I am not for the moment thinking of how much of what is best in art has been evoked and transfigured by its religious dedication, nor of the spiritual error of those who in later times robbed the stately and richly decorated churches in Norfolk and elsewhere of their original ornamentation. I am rather meaning this, that a sense of beauty is one of the highest capacities of our own souls, and that it is the privilege of the Church to sanctify and exalt all that is greatest in man, and to shed some of the glory of the eternal world about the art of man's inspired device.

Beauty is one of the three existences which stand before us in independent reality, instinctively recognized *by the soul* as not being creations of its own but as being great Sovereign Powers outside itself, to whom it renders a responsive homage. Truth, Right, Beauty, these three exist from God ; they abide and we bow to them ; and the more humbly and unreservedly we do so, the more we are uplifted. " He that wonders shall reign," so is our Lord said to have spoken, and such wonder, such admiration, of these three great things raises us towards them. Whatever perversion there may be in our reception of them, Truth, Right, and Beauty are windows opening towards Heaven through which the light of the Revelation of God reaches us. To follow the right, to seek the truth, to love the beautiful, obviously these are means of grace. But we often forget it ; and, to give an example, both in the realm of truth and of beauty, we forget how much our books, like good friends, can help us along the path that God has set before us. We must, no doubt, *choose* what we read, wisely and well : many of us may deplore the flood of poor or degrading literature that the careless have now put within their easy reach. But I am speaking of the literature that is full of, and is the expression of, beauty and truth ; and I say that such work, such art, does lift men's intellects and souls to God.

But if beauty and truth are allied, so are beauty and right ; and he must be a man of slow imagination who neither sees the grace of lovely home life where people move in fair surroundings, nor feels the beautiful appeal of many a gallant act of unselfishness shown by those who live in poor houses and unpromising environment. From such a home did John Crome emerge to eventual fame ; and we rejoice to know that while few may have his talent directly to increase the beautiful treasures of the world, many are every day exhibiting, in spite of temptation, and sordid homes, the lily-like beauty of generous, brave, chaste, and loving lives ; and many too the beauty of patient courageous suffering. Truth, Right, Beauty, these touch the life of man and draw it to themselves and draw it to God. And they find their centre in Him Who has declared Himself the Way— and at least that includes the right way for men to advance towards God and that must mean right conduct—the Way and the Truth and the Life : in Him Who also spoke of Himself as the Good, the Beautiful Shepherd. And as we seek the better to grasp this threefold strand, it is He Who by His own power will strengthen our grasp upon it. . . .

If these great celebrations are to teach us lessons for life that reach further than the happy commemoration of the founder of the Norwich school of painters, I would venture to suggest to you these things : First, that we should make every effort that we can to bring such charm and nobility into our own lives and the lives of others, that even in outward demeanour, dress, and bearing there should be some of the graciousness which counts for much in human intercourse. Secondly, that we should strive to introduce simple beauty by simple art into the homes of our less fortunate fellows. Thirdly, that we should not think it a matter of no importance whether the houses and the rooms in which they dwell are sweet and inviting and built with taste and individual attractiveness—for this need involve no costly extravagance. Believe me, public opinion counts for much in a matter of this kind, as indeed it does in the effort to see that on the stage and in the house of entertainment the degradation of art should not be substituted for its beauty. And then that in our own life we should try to follow the example of Goethe, who is reported to have said, " Look every day at something first-rate—a poem, a picture, a statue, the life of a great man," and holding fast to all the light that has come to us through the apprehension and the welcome of Right, Truth, and Beauty, ask, in the words he spoke on his death-bed, that even for this life there may be given unto us " Light, more light." So shall we keep ourselves from being engrossed in sordid details, with no fresh air of beauty, no radiance of light to sweeten, brighten, and cheer the day. Lastly, let us remember that the disciple whom Jesus loved saw in all the humiliation of His earthly life the glory shining through ; and that we on our part, even in those ordinary and uninspiring details of busy occupation, are called to follow in the bright footsteps of Him Who lived His life among men full of grace and truth—full of grace and truth.

XIX

BEAUTY IN WORSHIP [1]

" He is altogether lovely."—Song of Songs v. 16

I AM pleased to be with you to-day for this service, which, in thanksgiving to God, marks a further stage in the constant beautification of your noble church. Bit by bit, with unceasing liberality, the people of this generation have tried in their time to catch the spirit of your founders, and to restore the glory of their handiwork.

And to-day, I know it, the hearts of some of you are filled not only with pride in the growing glory of this House of God, not only with delight in being allowed to follow in the footsteps of the great church builders of the past, but with a yet more tender and personal sentiment. Some of these admirable figures are given in memory of absent friends, still present in the Communion of Saints, whose invisible but real fellowship still is felt by those to whom they are now as dear as ever. Truly we feel such nearness to Christ as often as we disentangle our spirits from the preoccupations of this life, and in the words of to-day's precious collect are " in heart exalted unto the same place whither our Saviour Christ is gone before," the Lord both of the dead and living, gone before to prepare a place for our friends whom He has taken to Himself, and for us when we are called to rejoin them.

We know that no gifts of ours can enhance the honour of God : " For all the beasts of the forest are mine : and so are the cattle upon a thousand hills." " If I be hungry, I will not tell thee : for the whole

---

[1] A sermon preached in the Church of St. Mary and St. Thomas, Wymondham, May 29th, 1927, at the dedication of new work in the church.

world is mine, and all that is therein. . . . Offer unto
God thanksgiving : and pay thy vows unto the most
highest."

Yes, but in making such gifts to His temple we do
offer unto God thanksgiving, and in the adornment of
His holy place we are openly showing the reverence of
our hearts ; inward adoration finds an expression in
the beautification of the Sanctuary. True beauty is
the natural language of true worship in spirit and
truth. It is easy to say this in this diocese justly
famous for its wonderful churches, great and small.

True beauty in worship, as elsewhere, touches deep,
and lifts to the heights ; it is not a superficial or shallow
sense or emotion. For beauty, genuine beauty, will
only reveal itself to one who has the eyes to see it
and to portray. The photographer cannot rival the
painter, nor the builder the architect. The true artist
of the beautiful has a gift of insight to see beneath
the surface ; whether he contemplates persons or
objects, he must see with the eye of the soul that can
pierce through and descry the inner meaning and grace
which the outward form half hides and half discloses.

There have been times when men have, of set
purpose, tried to remove beauty from worship and
from life. Look at the defacement of our cathedrals.
But can we really doubt that beauty *is* a part of God's
will or that a man genuinely developed must respond
to it ? There is a sacramental value leading us
Godward in all beauty, the beauty of a glorious land-
scape, of the heavens above and the earth beneath, the
spreading ocean, the splendour of the morning as it
dawns on the hills, the beauty of men's creative art,
the beauty of a lovely countenance and the grace of
the human form, the girl in the first bloom of youth or
the fine carriage of distinguished age.

This brings us to inquire about the Lord Himself.
Do His words and actions tell on the side of beauty or
against it, or are they indifferent to it ? His actions

must constantly have involved making what was foul and ugly fresh and fair as His voice or His hand touched the suffering, the paralysed, the blind. What joy to see the beauty returning to the countenance ! And as for His words, can we not learn that Our Lord was sensitive to beauty ? We may answer emphatically " Yes " if it was the beauty of God's creation which was very good ; or the beauty of holiness. " Consider the lilies of the field," these, as symbols of the Father's love and care, were holy and beautiful in His eyes and in their unsought charm, more beautiful than Solomon in all his glory. Think, too, of the way in which, describing Himself as the Good Shepherd, He chose that word for " good " which meant the " beautiful " as well. And I believe we may find corroboration in His love of nature, His parables, that came from the out-of-doors, His reference to the growing trees and the vines, the waving corn, the skies above. All these are touches which show that He was not indifferent to those sights and scents and sounds that stir the feeling of beauty in our hearts when we are out and about in the sweet countryside.

But Our Lord knew and cared little for luxurious workmanship which, in its gorgeous ornamentation yet carried with it no symbol of the love of God. He spoke as one aloof from king's houses. As He looked from the Mount of Olives upon Jerusalem He was not fascinated by the marvellous building and decoration of the temple, embellished for a political purpose, even if it looked like " a dream of gold and snow." " Seest thou these great buildings ? There shall not be one stone left upon another." It was only, I suppose, twice in His life that He entered any magnificent house ; He stood, we know, a prisoner before Herod with no eyes to look upon the mean princeling's halls as anything but ugly and hateful ; for they ministered to one who cared for show and not for God. And when on that same day He stood upon the rich mosaic of the pavement of Pilate's Prætorium, it was only to stain it with drops of blood.

Our Lord seems to teach us that beauty is real to those who welcome it as a beam of radiance from God, for those who look upwards, "still upward," up " to the land of beauty where things of beauty meet." Such as these beauty inspires with a heavenly yearning where words fail—indeed " there is neither speech nor language," but its voices are plainly heard : it touches the secret places of the heart, going far deeper than any human expression, any form of literature or art, can reveal.

" Behold the man," so said Pilate : " a man of sorrows and acquainted with grief." Was it these words that caused the early Christians to represent the Lord as without beauty ? Before we reply to this question which we may be allowed to ask on a day when we have been dedicating these wondrous carved figures of some of His servants, designed and elaborated with exquisite skill, we must first recall the fact that the present conventional portrait of Christ has no authority.   Then we go on to applaud the reticence of Holy Scripture, which here, as often elsewhere, does not satisfy such a really irrelevant inquiry. For we do not want to look back to find Christ as He was ; we want to see Him as He is now present to the eye of faith, our living Lord.   But well knowing that the point is of no crucial value, I venture to repeat the question, " Was Christ really without form or comeliness ? " You can, I believe, quote Fathers of the ancient Church who would have said, " Yes."   Dean Milman tells the whole tale.   And though we love to think of the picture of the Lord in the catacombs almost like a young Apollo with a sheep, some say a goat, upon His shoulders, certainly the earliest portraiture does represent the Lord without grace or beauty. But we can scarcely believe that this is not a misrepresentation.   We know that for us He humbled Himself and for our sake His visage was so marred more than any man. But He Who at His Incarnation sinlessly took upon Himself the form of man, He Who was and is the Representative Man, the sum and crown of the human race at its best and loftiest, we cannot believe that *He* was just an average man in appearance ; rather we judge that He showed the highest beauty of our manhood without, as well as within. It is an injury inflicted on Christian faith and worship when Christ is represented in stone or glass or canvas in the hour of His bitterest torture with an outward humiliation that is unrelieved by the inherent eternal glory. For we must never think of the Cross of Christ without thinking of the Divine Majesty of Him Who, as the quaint Latin phrases it, reigned from the tree. The Cross of shame was the scene of Christ's sacrifice, the way to His victory ; but, as we stand beneath it, we must look on to the Resurrection which actually proclaimed Him Victor and showed the triumph of the Cross. He was indeed obedient unto death, even the death of the Cross. But if this Divine Glory shone through His Passion, we may believe that it rested upon a perfect beauty of human face and form belonging to the Perfect Son of Man, the adorable Son of God, in all His suffering still beautiful in the eyes of the heavenly hosts and to the Father on His sapphire throne, still beautiful in the eyes of men : ever the same, beautiful in look and word and work ; beautiful in life, beautiful in death ; beautiful in His Resurrection and Ascension as He lifted up His pierced hands to give to His disciples His final blessing ; beautiful beyond compare, the chiefest among ten thousand, and altogether lovely.

XX

IDEALS OF CHRISTIAN MARRIAGE [1]

I ALWAYS like it that our Prayer Book marks the joy of the wedding day by saying in so many words that the bride and bridegroom are to be supported in the Marriage Service by their friends and neighbours. Rightly you are here to wish them God-speed in their new life of united love, and you have already sanctified your wish by changing it into prayer. And you are representatives of a far larger number of friends—friends whom distances and partings never affect, who on both sides of the Atlantic and away across Europe have heard or will hear of the glad news of to-day with much joy. What can surpass the sacred bliss of a happy wedding day ?

Many people to-day take the view that marriage is a personal matter between one man and one woman, and that those two, and those two only, are concerned with its beginning, and with its end or dissolution. They forget that there is always a third party concerned in the matter, namely, the State, which is the guardian of all the people and their homes, the protector of the children of a marriage and the upholder of our public standards. It is, here as elsewhere, the champion of lawful rights and relations. It carefully watches over the commencement, the continuance, the conclusion of marriage.

In the heart of the devout Christian there is yet One more Person who has a chief place, all His own, in a happy wedding.

To-day we who are gathered here are thinking of the Lord Christ, present with us to hallow this union in the

[1] A sermon preached at 1 Carlton House Terrace, London, on July 14th, 1931, at the marriage of Mr. Albert Jay Wright with Miss Tatiana Mosolova.

fullness of its emotions and comfort and peace and comradeship. Here we are taking our part in what our Prayer Book rightly calls Holy Matrimony, and the thought of the Lord Christ Himself in our midst in all the power of His endless life and the recollection of the teaching of His Apostles set a new value upon marriage. The last wonderful prayer speaks of the love of Christ for His Church, and it is this reference to Christ's love, constantly renewed, that brings the best out of married life and love. Its joys are consecrated if they are received from Him and laid with thanksgiving at His feet. Its cares are lightened if husband and wife share them together, and together lean on His arm for help and together look up into His face for counsel and comfort, for it is the Face of One Who is perfect Wisdom, perfect Love, and the perfect Way of Life. To fall or to fail to carry out His Will would be a failure that would grieve not only the partners in a marriage themselves, it would grieve the Lord Himself Who had joined them in one in His Own Name. He is ever a Third in their daily companionship, and apart from Him it could never reach its highest ideal. He it is Who makes the outward affection the symbol of a loftier holy union ; at Christ's touch all life, and of course not least in its most beautiful phases, is made sacramental and lifted up to the heavenly places.

Let us then pray for such things for our two friends this morning. May we ourselves see more and more clearly the glory of a true holy marriage and ask that its purest and most celestial gifts may be the lasting, the growing, and the inalienable treasure of the bride and bridegroom of to-day. Oh, may they ever come nearer and nearer to the best in one another as they come nearer to Christ, each offering the best that he, that she, can by God's grace attain to the other, and each finding the best in the other as they make their love more and more worthy to be compared with the love of Christ for His Bride the Church.

XXI

FELLOWSHIP WITH THE DEPARTED [1]

" Wherefore seeing we also are compassed about with so great a
cloud of witnesses . . . let us run with patience the race that is
set before us."—Heb. xii. 1

IT is, I suppose, a common instinct that leads us
to wish to be present during the last hours of the
life of those whom we love. We are distressed if we
do not receive in time the hasty summons. If we
arrive too late, we seem to have suffered a loss that
cannot be repaired, and, even so, there are some of us
who hasten to the quiet chamber where our dear one
has been laid, in order that we may see the frail frame
once more before it is finally removed from our sight.
In the way in which we all desire to enjoy the company
of our friends till the very last before they leave our
shores when they are starting for far lands, and to
wish them God-speed for their voyage, as we respectfully wish it to two royal travellers [2] this morning starting
on their long journey of imperial import, even so it is,
only in an intensified degree, when our friends are
parting from us on their way to " the undiscovered
country from whose bourne no traveller returns." At
all such times we wish to hear the last words, to catch
the last smile, to clasp the hand for the last time, to
exchange a mutual farewell ; yes, and we enter that
silent room as if we thus could postpone the breaking
of the happy companionship which on earth we really
know is now over for ever, almost deceiving ourselves
by the first change which may have brought a fresh
beauty to the face which we loved, making it look
younger, as it was, perhaps, in those days of long ago,

[1] A sermon preached in Sandringham Church October 29th,
1911.
[2] Their Majesties were shortly leaving for India.

when between us two for the first time eye spoke to eye
and heart to heart, fondly deceiving ourselves, I say,
as we gaze with the eyes of him

> Who hath bent him o'er the dead,
> Ere the first day of death is fled
>
> .   .   .   .   .
>
> (Before Decay's effacing fingers
> Have swept the lines where beauty lingers),
> And mark'd the mild angelic air,
> The rapture of repose that's there,
> The fix'd yet tender traits that streak
> The languor of the placid cheek.
>
> .   .   .   .   .
>
> Some moments, ay, one treacherous hour,
> Who still might doubt the tyrant's power,
> So fair, so calm, so softly seal'd,
> The first, last look by death reveal'd.

But however natural is this our conduct in the presence
of illness and death, I doubt whether usually we are the
gainers thereby ; for, though now and again we may
win some last interchange of recognition, or that last
sweet gleam upon the countenance, more generally it
only means that we are brought to see our friends in
the extremity of suffering, when the mind is already far
away, and that the last impression that we have is
not wholly one of peace but also one of sorrow and
distress.

And from this a further misfortune frequently
follows, that when we recall our dearest to our minds,
we think of them as we last saw them in discomfort
or pain, and exclude from our hearts the real true self
in all the glory of happy manly strength, or in the
charm of living womanly grace, and we cling to the
spot where their mortal remains are laid, and we think
of them as they were in death and not in life ; we
think of them, to use St. Paul's phrase, not " in power
but in weakness." Even our very conceptions of
them as they now are, that is, as we picture them
present with the Lord, are marred by the thought of

the " grave and gate of death " through which they
have entered upon this holy fellowship.

Now the touching thoughts connected with these
memorials, which we are dedicating in memory of the
great King to-day, are not spoilt by any weakening
reminiscences of this kind.   This church is not connected with his death but with his life ; we love to
think of him as he would enter it ; we watch him taking
his own seat at the end of the pew ; we see him with
our mind's eye once more here in all the fine vigour of
his manhood.

And we go on to recall his attachment to this place
and all that is in it ; how he personally interested
himself in every detail, and watched it all grow in its
beauty under his own hand.   He had from his earliest
days a high position to fill in the light of public life,
and especially in his later years ; the highest responsibilities to bear—and you know how nobly he bore
them—for his country's good.   The gaze, not only of
his great Empire, but of all Europe, nay, of the whole
world, was fixed on him who daily illustrated his own
intuitive sense of the right thing to do and to say in the
most varied circumstances and relationships, and by
his winning charm spread among others his own devotion to peace and good-will among all men at home and
abroad.   If ever there was a life that occupied a
conspicuous central station it was his.   But this was
his country home, and here more than anywhere else
he could throw off the cares of State, as he found
himself among his own people—those people who were
united to him, not merely with the loyalty, respect,
and devotion which in his wide dominions characterized
all his subjects, but who turned to him with a personal,
individual affection of their own, and were never
disappointed, as they sought in him, not only their
noble and honoured King, but their tender-hearted
squire, their generous, sympathetic friend.   They are
those who have united together to erect this memorial

in this church, so sacredly identified with his family life and with their own—some of them in high stations, one in the highest, some of them of humbler degree, but all united, prince and peasant together, in the bond of love for him who has gone. We are glad that so many of them are present with us to-day ; and we know that others who are absent are with us in heart —one very specially, so long the faithful servant of his late master, and now of her to whom all hearts go out in humble sympathy ; one who on his sick bed as an old man shows the heroism which won the young man his V.C. ; one to whom Sandringham is as dear as he is dear to Sandringham.[1]

On a pathetic occasion a famous sermon was preached in this church on Recognition in Eternity ; to-day I would ask you, my brethren, to learn from one great passage of Holy Scripture that we need not wait for the eternity to come, before we can be sure that our dear ones who have passed into the other world know us still, and watch us still.

The writer of the great epistle from which my text has been taken has just given a glorious muster-roll of the old saints of God. And now he calls before his mind one of the great theatres so common in the ancient world—their appearance is not unfamiliar. Many of you have seen pictures of the Colosseum in Rome, which was said to hold more than eighty thousand spectators ; some of us have stood within those huge walls, magnificent in their naked ruins. Some such great theatre rises before the eyes of the author of our text ; he pictures us as struggling in it, competing for the prize, doing our best to win our race. He fills the rising tiers and tiers of seats with a vast concourse of those who have passed from this world to the next—" a great cloud," he calls them. " We are compassed about with a great cloud "—of what ? Of spectators ? Yes, but far more than spectators ;

[1] Sir Dighton Probyn.

witnesses they are, too—witnesses to the power in
which they once conquered when they were placed
where we are now.   These witnesses are all about us ;
they are watching ; they care.   We know how, in a
contest, the vigour of a team is stimulated when they
hear the shouts of those who look on, and, by calling
the name which they all alike are proud to bear, urge
them to do their best ; so here is it as if we could
actually listen to the voices from this great cloud—
yes, and among them hear, with a personal appeal,
some dearest voice of all to us, " the sound of a voice
that is still "—and all this to stimulate us to do as
much as they did, to do even more : to be worthy of
the one cause which in their day was entrusted to
them, in ours to us.

We are indeed wise not to think of them as if their
continued brotherhood was independent of Him who
was not ashamed to call us and them His brethren.   It
is because we and they are alike with Christ that we
enter into the lives of one another ; He is the point of
union.   And we must remember that we are necessarily
using figurative language when we describe their nearness to us in terms borrowed from earthly associations ;
we have no powers to describe the manner in the
connexion of this world and its denizens with the other
world and those who are in it.   But if the manner cannot
be expressed, the fellowship itself, centred in Christ, is
certain.   And as we now bear our part, as in our turn we,
too, desire out of weakness to be made strong, it cheers
us to remember that the unseen world, even though
in a way we cannot yet define, is very close to us,
and that it is filled with Christ's people many of whom
we ourselves have loved—we love.   As we put forth
our efforts, and run hither and thither in the dangerous
arena of our life, they are calling to us to look up again
and again from the things " upon earth, where moth
and rust doth corrupt," to our real treasure in heaven,
of which indeed they themselves are a true part.

They are not, they could not wish to be, independent of us ; for, as we read in the preceding verse, " they without us shall not be made perfect."   They have not left us ; we are really not alone ; and we enrich all our life by already making our own in practical daily duty the unseen but not unfelt companionship of this " great cloud of witnesses," even if the brightest hope of all is still before us to gladden us in the days to come long hence, when

> The night is gone ;
> And with the morn those angel faces smile,
> Which we have loved long since, and lost awhile.

EPILOGUE

IN this selection of sermons I have tried to show some of the bearings of our Faith in Christ upon various aspects of English life. Except in the titles of some sermons I have not used the word " religion " to any great extent, because of its indeterminate or even evasive character. It is a popular word, and since the War it has found a considerable vogue, perhaps because it commits those who use it to very little. It need indicate no more than a vague aspiration, and it sometimes offers merely a field for argument. Faith in Christ is different. It is historic and personal, and makes definite claims upon those who hold it in sincerity. It opens their eyes, it masters their characters, it occupies their hearts.

Now, this Faith in the Divine Christ by its very nature touches the whole man and reaches to the whole of life. No public or domestic or private area of thought or action is beyond its influence and control. And it has been the aim of these sermons to bring some of the primary interests of our English life into relation with this Faith.

I am assured that our English devotion and belief have an individuality of their own. The Christian Faith evokes a variety of response in different lands and among different races. We believe that as each fresh people is brought into vital contact with the Living Christ it will enrich the common treasury by making its own contribution of view and conduct. The riches of Christ are " unsearchable," and every new group of believers, exploring for itself, will make new discoveries about Him, and render its homage. Nothing, for example, could be worse than that we should make the double mistake of imposing stereotyped Western forms of theology or worship on the

East, and of expecting in return a discipleship which exactly repeats our own idiom.

I have never hesitated to maintain that, as we are English men and women, so our Faith in Christ runs along British lines. Some would have us look abroad for our ideals. But neither in our ordinary ways of seeing and doing things, nor in our spiritual outlook, are we likely to be at home with the manner of Latin countries. Even in the Prayer Book discussions I felt that it was the English side of the issue which was all important. Of course, this immediately led on to doctrinal controversy, for those who maintain truth (as they see it) will be rejecting error (as they see it) and calling it by that name. But it was the strong and independent English hold upon the truth of Christ, justifying itself by the tests of Holy Scripture, so it seemed to me, which must be safeguarded.

Without being pharisaical and certainly welcoming, as I just said, every illumination of our Faith which can come from any quarter, we may thank God for the light which He has shown to us as individuals and as a nation. This light is not meant for selfish enjoyment and comfort ; it carries a clear duty with it— to consecrate ourselves, and, so far as may be, our generation, with all that we have, to the worship and the service of Almighty God. The British Empire has a Christian standing.

Here is a great theme which I hope may have been illustrated in some ways in *The Church and English Life*.

PRINTED BY
JARROLD AND SONS LTD.
NORWICH